CHILDREN'S
ATLAS

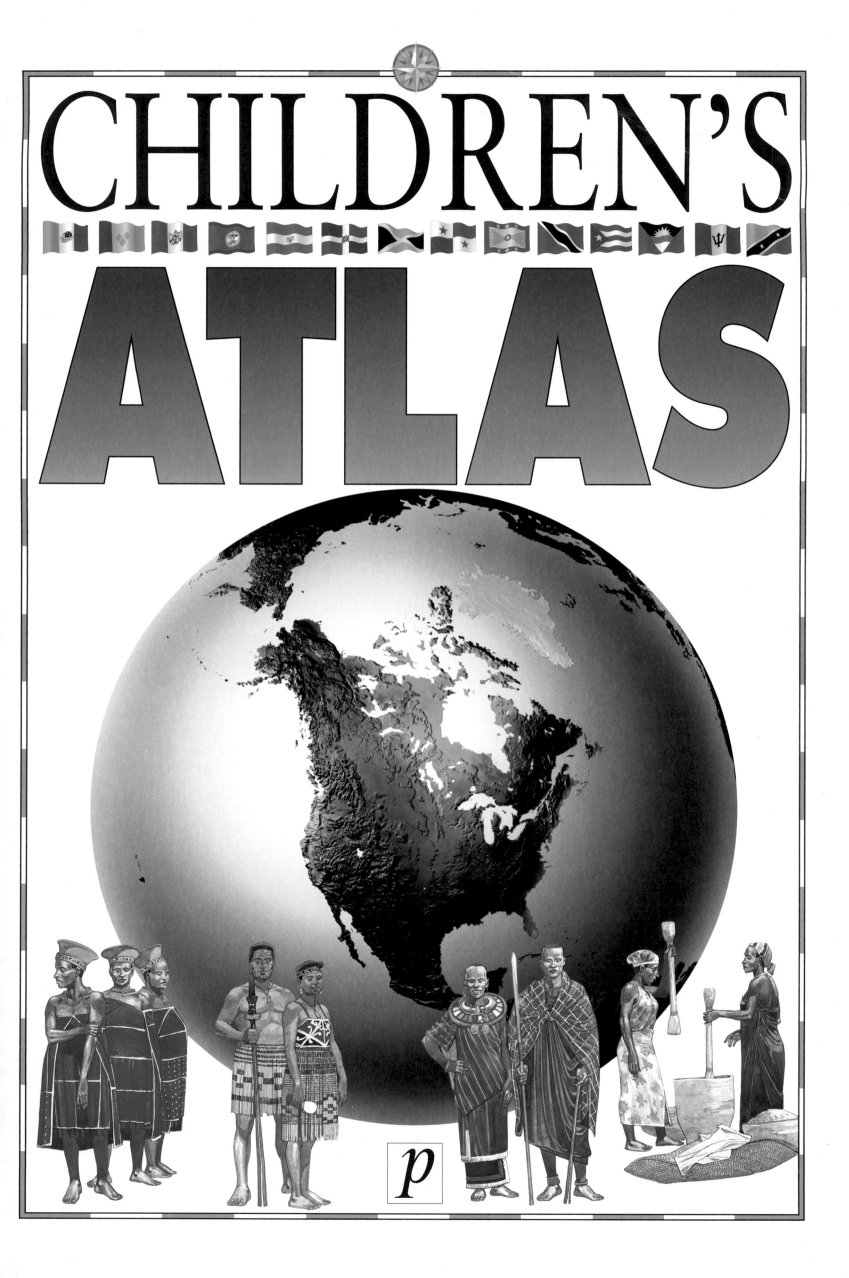

p

This is a Parragon Book
This edition published in 2000

Parragon
Queen Street House
4 Queen Street
Bath BA1 1HE, UK

2 4 6 8 10 9 7 5 3 1

Produced by
Miles Kelly Publishing Ltd
Unit 11, Bardfield Centre, Great Bardfield, Essex CM7 4SL
Copyright © Parragon 1998

British Library Cataloguing-in-Publication Data
A catalogue record for this book is available from the British Library.

Printed in Spain

ISBN 0-75253-944-2

Design: Full Steam Ahead

Cartographic Editor: Keith Lye

Cartography: Digital Wisdom

Artwork Commissioning: Branka Surla

Project Manager: Kate Miles

Additional help from Susanne Bull and Lynne French

Reprographics: DPI Colour Ltd

Cover Design: David West Children's Books

CONTENTS

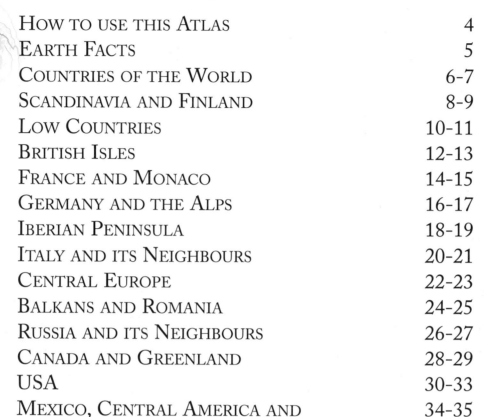

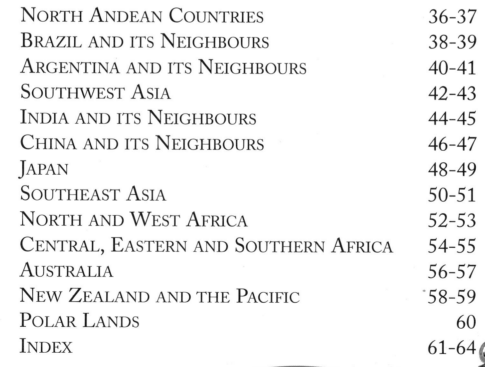

HOW TO USE THIS ATLAS

WELCOME TO THE PLANET EARTH! This atlas shows you the world we live in. An atlas is any large book of maps. Maps are plans which show the surface of a planet as if it was flat, instead of round. They show the lie of the land, the rivers and coastlines, mountains and seas.

Maps which just show the details of the landscape are called 'physical'. Maps which just show the borders of countries, states, counties or provinces are called 'political'. The maps in this book show the physical details of the land, but they show national borders and major cities as well. Maps use signs and symbols to give you more information. Look at the key to find out what they mean.

So how do you find the city or country you are looking for? First of all look up the name you want in the index on p.61. When you have found the right page, look for the name on the big map of the region. Next to each regional map, look for the little map which helps you to see at a glance which part of the world is being shown.

Next, read the words to find out more about the countries, the climate of the region, the peoples and how they live. Small boxes also give you key facts and figures about each of the countries. They tell you the area, the population size, the name of the capital city, the country's official language or languages and the currency, or type of money, used by the people there.

When you read about distant lands, it may help to compare them with where you live. Are they bigger or smaller, hotter or wetter, more crowded? You might use the maps to do a bit of detective work. Can you work out why most Australian cities are near the coast, or why most Canadian cities are in the south of the country?

Colours
On this map the different colours show you at a glance the physical features of the landscape. Each colour represents a type of geographic feature.

Spot the mountain
This symbol means 'mountain'. The mountain's name is printed next to it, along with the height of the summit above sea level. The height is given in metres.

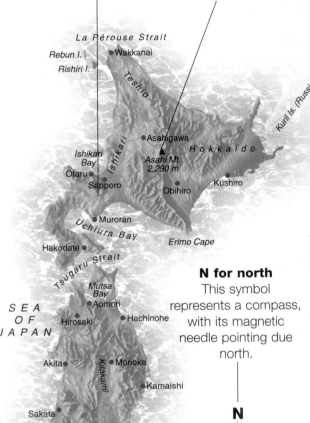

N for north
This symbol represents a compass, with its magnetic needle pointing due north.

Coastlines and borders
The borders of Japan are natural, because the country is made up of islands. Other countries may have land borders, marked by a line on the map.

Capital cities
The most important town in any country is called the capital city. This is very often the biggest town and is normally where the government makes the laws. Some capitals, however, are quite small.

Where in the world
If you want to find out where the regional map fits into a map of the whole world, check these small circular maps. The areas coloured in red show the location.

Key to symbols
- ■ Capitals
- ● Towns
- — Rivers
- ━ Borders
- Lakes
- Mountains

INTRODUCTION

EARTH FACTS

The world we live in is a huge ball of rock and metal spinning around, or rotating, in space. As the planet Earth rotates, it travels around the Sun, held on its path by a pulling force called gravity. The Earth is one of nine planets circling the Sun, and together they make up the Solar System.

When we see pictures of Earth taken from space, our planet appears blue, white and brown. The blue is the colour of the seas and oceans which cover over two-thirds of the Earth's surface. The swirling white patterns are the clouds – water vapour which hangs in the air, or atmosphere, surrounding the Earth's surface. The brown is the colour of the ground, which is divided into the Earth's landmasses or continents.

Photographs of the Earth's surface taken from space zoom in to show even more details – the world's great river systems, the high mountain ranges, the sprawling cities and the patchwork of crops that feed the hungry mouths of the world's population, which is expected to reach over 6,100 million by the year 2000.

PLANET EARTH
Circumference around the Equator: 40,075 kilometres
Circumference around the Poles: 40,008 kilometres
Diameter at the Equator: 12,756 kilometres
Surface area: About 510,000,000 square kilometres
Area covered by sea: 71 percent
Average distance from the Sun: 149,600,000 kilometres
Average distance from the Moon: 385,000 kilometres
Period of rotation: 23 hours 56 minutes
Speed of rotation: 1,660 kilometres per hour at the Equator
Period of revolution: 365 days 6 hours
Speed of revolution: 29.8 kilometres per second

The world's highest peak
Mount Everest or Qomolangma, between Nepal and China, is the highest point on the Earth's surface.

HIGHEST PEAKS
Mountain	Height	Location
Everest (Qomolangma)	8,848 m	China-Nepal
K2 (Qogir Feng)	8,611 m	India-Pakistan
Kanchenjunga	8,586 m	India-Nepal
Makalu 1	8,463 m	China-Nepal
Dhaulagiri 1	8,167 m	Nepal
Nanga Parbat	8,125 m	India
Annapurna 1	8,091 m	Nepal
Gosainthan (Xixabangma Feng)	8,012 m	China
Distaghil Sar	7,885 m	India
Nanda Devi	7,816 m	India

LONGEST RIVERS
River	Length	Location
Nile	6,670 km	North Africa
Amazon	6,448 km	South America
Chang Jiang (Yangtze)	6,300 km	Central China
Mississippi-Missouri-Red	6,020 km	North America
Yenisey-Angara-Selenga	5,540 km	Mongolia-Russia
Huang He	5,464 km	Northern China
Ob-Irtysh	5,409 km	Russia-Kazakhstan
Zaïre (Congo)	4,700 km	Central Africa
Lena-Kirenga	4,400 km	Russia
Mekong	4,350 km	Southeast Asia

LARGEST LAKES
Lake	Area	Location
Caspian Sea	371,800 sq km	Central Asia
Superior	82,103 sq km	USA-Canada
Victoria	69,484 sq km	East Africa
Aral Sea	65,500 sq km	Central Asia
Huron	59,569 sq km	USA-Canada
Michigan	57,757 sq km	USA-Canada
Tanganyika	32,893 sq km	East Africa
Baikal	31,449 sq km	Russia
Great Bear	31,328 sq km	Canada
Malawi	28,878 sq km	Southern Africa

LARGEST ISLANDS
Island	Area
Greenland	2,1830 sq km
New Guinea	821,000 sq km
Borneo	727,900 sq km
Madagascar	589,081 sq km
Baffin	509,214 sq km
Sumatra	431,982 sq km
Honshu	228,204 sq km
Great Britain	218,800 sq km
Victoria	212,200 sq km
Ellesmere	196,917 sq km

MAJOR WATERFALLS
Highest Waterfalls
	Height	Location
Angel Falls	979 m	Venezuela
Mardsalsfossen	774 m	Norway
Yosemite	739 m	United States

Waterfall	Greatest volume Volume	Location
Boyoma	17,000 cu m per sec	Dem. Rep. Congo (Zaïre)

OCEANS
Name	Area
Pacific	166,242,000 sq km
Atlantic	106,000,000 sq km
Indian	73,500,000 sq km
Arctic	14,350,000 sq km

COUNTRIES OF THE WORLD

To the glory of God
Places of worship vary greatly around the world. This Christian cathedral, St Basil's, was built in the 1500s in Moscow, capital of today's Russian Federation.

There are 192 countries in the world that are recognized as 'independent' nations, which means that they govern themselves. Many other lands are colonies or 'dependencies', which means that they are governed by other nations. The numbers change very often, as one country joins up with another one, or another splits up into separate nations. For example Eritrea was part of Ethiopia until 1991, when it broke away to become an independent nation.

Some countries are huge, some are tiny. The Russian Federation is the largest, with an area of 17,078,005 square kilometres. The smallest is Vatican City, at just 0.4 square kilometres. Some countries are home to just one people, while others are made up of many different peoples or ethnic groups, each with their own way of life and customs. Some peoples have no national borders of their own. For example the traditional homeland of the Kurdish people is divided between Turkey, Iraq and Iran.

The peoples of the world live very different lives. They have different faiths and beliefs, eat different foods and speak over 5000 different languages. Some people are very poor while others are very rich. However, the people on our planet also have many things in common. The spread of radio, television and other communications links in recent years has made the world a smaller place. Once it took years to travel around the world, but today we can get on a plane or keep in touch with each other at the push of a button.

Most of the world's countries are linked by agreements or treaties. Many European countries belong to the European Union, while African nations belong to the Organization of African Unity. Nearly all countries belong to the United Nations, which tries to prevent conflict and to build links between the world's nations.

Political power
These heads, cut from the rock at Mount Rushmore, USA, honour US presidents – George Washington, Thomas Jefferson, Theodore Roosevelt and Abraham Lincoln.

Trade and commerce
It is said that 'money makes the world go round'. These bright lights are in the Kowloon district of Hong Kong, a former British colony that returned to Chinese rule in 1997.

Cooking around the world
Pizza is made of a doughy pastry topped by cheese, tomato, vegetables, herbs and sausage. This Italian dish is now very popular in many parts of the world.

Save the wilderness
This ship is entering pack ice off the coast of Antarctica. Nobody lives in this freezing continent at the bottom of the world. It is one of the last few wild places on Earth.

Peoples and customs
Traditional body paint and costume are worn for this dance in Papua New Guinea. Regional dress has become less common around the world in recent years, but is still worn with pride for special ceremonies.

7

SCANDINAVIA AND FINLAND

FACT BOX

◆ **Denmark**
Area: 43,075 sq km
Population: 5,300,000
Capital: Copenhagen
Official language: Danish
Currency: Danish krone

◆ **Sweden**
Area: 449,790 sq km
Population: 8,000,000
Capital: Stockholm
Currency: Krona
Official language: Swedish

◆ **Norway**
Area: 323,895 sq km
Population: 4,400,000
Capital: Oslo
Official language: Norwegian
Currency: Norwegian krone

◆ **Finland**
Area: 337,030 sq km
Population: 5,100,000
Capital: Helsinki
Official language: Finnish
Currency: Markka

TWO PENINSULAS extend from northwestern Europe, shaped rather like the claws of a crab. The southern peninsula, extending from Germany, is called Jutland.

Together with a chain of islands which includes Fyn, Sjælland, and Lolland, Jutland makes up the nation of **Denmark**. Most of Denmark is flat and low-lying, a country of green farmland. It exports bacon and dairy products.

Across the windy channels of Sgagerrak and Kattegat, between the North and Baltic Seas, lies the long northern peninsula occupied by **Sweden** and **Norway**. This is a land shaped by movements of ice in prehistoric times. Glaciers carved out the deep sea inlets called fjords along its ragged western coast. Ranges of mountains run down the peninsula like a backbone. They descend to a land of forests, bogs and thousands of lakes.

Summers can be warm, but winters are bitterly cold, with heavy snow. Norway lives by fishing and its North Sea rigs make it Western Europe's largest producer of oil and natural gas. Sweden is a major exporter of timber, paper, wooden furniture and motor vehicles.

The three nations of Denmark, Sweden and Norway form the region of Scandinavia. It was from here that the seafarers known as Vikings set out about 1,200 years ago. The Vikings raided and settled the coasts of Western Europe, traded in Russia and the Middle East, settled Iceland and Greenland and even reached North America. Today's Danes, Swedes and Norwegians are all closely related, as are the Germanic languages that they speak.

The Arctic lands of northern Scandinavia are home to the Saami (or Lapps), a people who traditionally lived by herding reindeer. Their neighbours are the Finns and the Russians.

Finland is a land of lakes, with coasts on the Gulfs of Bothnia and Finland. Its forests make it a leading producer of wood pulp and paper. Helsinki is the capital.

FINLAND

ICELAND

RUSSIA

ICELAND

Raufarhöfn
Kópasker
Vopnafjördur
Seyhisfjördur
Neskaupstadur
Eskifjördur
Búdir
Djúpivogur
Jökulsá á Fjöllum
Höfn
Grímsey
Húsavík
Hvannadalshnúkur 2,119m
Myvatn
Skálfandafljót
Akureyri
VATNAJÖKULL
Ólafsfjördur
Saudárkrókur
VATNAJÖKULL
Hólmavík
Blanda
HOFSJÖKULL
Thingeyri
Blönduós
Porisvatn
Hekla 1,491 m
Vík
Hvitá
Surtsey
Isafjördur
Stykkishólmur
LANGJÖKULL
MYRDALSJÖKULL
Breidafjördur
Vatneyri
Hvitá
Vestmannaeyjar
Ólafsvik
Borgarnes
Pingvallavatn
Heimaey
Akranes
Reykjavik
Stokkseyri
Keflavík

North Cape
Vadsø
Kirkenes
Polmak
Utsjoki
Inarijärvi
Hammerfest
Karasjok
Enontekiö
Sodankylö
Pelkosenniemi
Rovaniemi
Alta
Mt. Haltia 1,324m
Oulu
Tornio
Kemi
Tromsø
Kiruna
Vittangi
Gällivare
Luleå
Piteä
Mt. Kebnekaise 2,111m
Jokkmokk
Boden
Narvik
Skellefte
LOFOTEN VESTERÅLEN
Bodø
Sorsele
Mosjøen
Storuman

8

N

FINLAND

Joensuu
Outokumpu
Kuopio
Jyväskylä
Kokkola
Jakobstad
Kouvola
Kotka
Lahti
Seinäjoki
Vaasa
Tampere
Hämeenlinna
Hyvinkää
Helsinki
Turku
Pori
Rauma
Mariehamn
ÅLAND

Bygdeå
Umeå
Dorotea
Ornsköldsvik
Kramfors
Sundsvall
Östersund
Ljusdal
Hudiksvall
Söderhamn
Bollnäs
Gävle
Falun
Mora
Borlänge
Västerdal
Uppsala
Västerås
Eskilstuna
Örebro
Norrköping
Linköping
Visby
Västervik
Borgholm
GOTLAND
ÖLAND
Kalmar
Karlskrona
Ronne
Bornholm

Gulf of Bothnia

BALTIC SEA

SWEDEN

🏳 SWEDEN

Stockholm, the heart of Sweden
The Swedish capital, Stockholm, is built between Lake Mälar and the Baltic Sea. The city covers several islands. It includes the mediaeval Old Town, merchants' houses from the 1900s and many modern factories and offices.

People of the Arctic
The Saami people live in Lapland, a region which extends right across the Scandinavian Arctic. Traditionally they are a nomadic people, who follow their herds of reindeer.

NORWEGIAN SEA

Steinkjer
Trondheim
Røros
Sunndalsøra
Kristiansund
Ålesund
Dombås
Lillehammer
Gjøvik
Voss
Bergen
Uskedal
Haugesund
Stavanger
Egersund
Särna
▲ *Galdhøpiggen 2,469m*
Oslo
Drammen
Skien
Fredrikstad
Larvik
Strömstad
Arendal
Kristiansand
Mandal

Stockholm
Södertälje
Karlstad
Vänern
Trollhättan
Uddevalla
Göteborg
Boras
Jönköping
Vättern
Växjö
Halmstad
Helsingborg
Kristianstad
Malmö
Ystad
Trelleborg

NORWAY

🏳 NORWAY

Skagerrak

Kattegat

Ålborg
Holstebro
Viborg
Randers
Århus
Horsens
Esbjerg
Kolding
Odense
JUTLAND
Copenhagen

DENMARK

🏳 DENMARK

GERMANY

The Little Mermaid
This bronze statue in the Danish capital, Copenhagen, shows a character from one of the children's stories by Hans Christian Andersen (1805-75). Andersen created some of the world's best loved fairy tales.

LOW COUNTRIES

FACT BOX

◆ **Netherlands**
Area: 41,160 sq km
Population: 15,600,000
Capital: Amsterdam
Official language: Dutch
Currency: Guilder

◆ **Belgium**
Area: 30,520 sq km
Population: 10,200,000
Capital: Brussels
Official languages: Flemish, French
Currency: Belgian franc

◆ **Luxembourg**
Area: 2,585 sq km
Population: 400,000
Capital: Luxembourg
Official language: French, German, Letzebuergesch
Currency: Luxembourg franc

THE COUNTRY OF THE NETHERLANDS is sometimes called Holland, but that is really the name of just two of its provinces, North and South Holland. This is a very flat, low-lying part of northern Europe. Long barriers and sea walls have been built to protect the countryside from North Sea floods. Large areas of land called polders have been reclaimed from the sea over the ages.

After a period under Spanish rule, the **Netherlands** became wealthy in the 1600s by trading with Southeast Asia. Its capital city, Amsterdam, still has many beautiful old houses and canals dating back to this golden age. The Netherlands today remain a centre of commerce, exporting bulbs and cut flowers, vegetables and dairy products, especially cheese, and also electrical goods. Rotterdam is the world's busiest seaport. Peoples of the Netherlands include the Dutch and the Frisians, as well as people whose families came from former Dutch colonies in Indonesia and Surinam.

The Flemish people of **Belgium** are closely related to the Dutch and their two languages are very similar. Belgium is also home to a French-speaking people, the Walloons, who mostly live in the south of the country. Much of the countryside in Belgium is also low and flat, but the land rises to the wooded hills of the Ardennes in the south. The country is heavily industrialized, and is also known for its fine foods – chocolates, pâtés, hams and traditional beers.

Luxembourg is a tiny country, a survivor of the age when most of Europe was divided into little states, principalities and duchies. However, modern industry and banking have made Luxembourg wealthy and successful. The people of Luxembourg speak French, German and a local language called Letzebuergesch.

The three countries have close ties. In 1948, after the terrible years of World War II (1939–45), Belgium, the Netherlands and Luxembourg set up an economic union called 'Benelux'. In 1957 they went on to what is now the European Union (EU).

Bruges skyline
The brick gables of old merchants' houses make a pleasing skyline in many historical towns of the Lowlands. Bruges has been famous through the ages for its lacemaking. The city is linked by canal to the seaport of Zeebrugge.

Wetlands butterfly
The Large Copper butterfly is on the endangered species list in both Belgium and the Netherlands. The butterfly thrives in flooded fields. Its caterpillar can survive underwater for many weeks. However draining of wetlands by farmers and roadbuilders threatens its survival.

NETHERLANDS

Enschede • Almelo • Emmen • Assen • Groningen • Meppel • Zwolle • Leeuwarden • Sneek • North-East Polder • Flevoland Polder • Markerwaard Polder (planned) • IJsselmeer • Waddenzee • West Frisian Islands • Ameland • Terscheling • Vlieland • Texel • Barrier Dam • Alkmaar • Zaanstad • Haarlem • ■ Amsterdam • Hilversum

'When it's spring again...'
The classic Dutch landscape includes fields of brilliantly coloured tulips and old-fashioned windmills. Both attract the tourists and are seen here near the town of Haarlem.

Dutch cheese
Another popular attraction in the Netherlands is the cheese market at Alkmaar. The Netherlands exports mild cheeses such as Edam and Gouda around the world.

GERMANY

Arnhem

Nijmegen
Waal

s'Hertogenbosch
Maas

Venlo

Eindhoven

Genk

Hasselt

Heerlen
Maastricht

Vaalserberg
321m

Verviers

Spa

Botrange
694m

GERMANY

LUXEMBOURG

Luxembourg

Esch-sur-Alzette

Burgplatz
559m

Lek

Delft

Rotterdam
Dordrecht

Breda
Tilburg

Antwerp

Mechelen

Leuven
(Louvain)

Waterloo

Liège

Meuse

Huy

Namur
Sambre

Charleroi

Dinant

ARDENNES
MOUNTAINS

Bastogne

Libramont

LUXEMBOURG

Oosterschelde

Vlissingen

Westerschelde

St. Niklaas

Brussels

BELGIUM

Aalst

La Louvière

Mons

Ghent

Schelde

Tournai

Zeebrugge

Bruges

Kortijk

Roeslare

Ostend

NETHERLANDS

N

BELGIUM

The future – 1958 style
This strange looking landmark is the Atomium. It was built for the World Fair held in Brussels in 1958 and was meant to be a symbol of a new age of atomic science and technology.

FRANCE

BRITISH ISLES

FACT BOX

◆ **United Kingdom:
England, Scotland, Wales,
N. Ireland**
 Area: 242,480 sq km
 Population: 58,000,000
 Official language: English
 Currency: Sterling pound

◆ **England**
 Area: 130,420 sq km
 Population: 48,675,119
 Capital: London
 Official language: English
 Currency: Sterling pound

◆ **Scotland**
 Area: 77,170 sq km
 Population: 5,111,000
 Capital: Edinburgh
 Official language: English
 Currency: Sterling pound

◆ **Wales**
 Area: 20,770 sq km
 Population: 2,899,000
 Capital: Cardiff
 Official language: Welsh,
  English
 Currency: Sterling pound

◆ **Northern Ireland**
 Area: 74,120 sq km
 Population: 1,610,000
 Capital: Belfast
 Official language: English
 Currency: Sterling pound

◆ **Republic of Ireland**
 Area: 70,283 sq km
 Population: 3,552,000
 Capital: Dublin
 Official language: English, Irish
 Currency: Irish pound (punt)

THE BRITISH ISLES lie off the northwestern coast of Europe, between the shallow waters of the North Sea and the stormy Atlantic Ocean. Their western shores are warmed by an ocean current called the North Atlantic Drift. The climate is mild, with a high rainfall in the west.

The largest island is called **Great Britain,** and its three countries (**England, Scotland** and **Wales**) are joined together within a United Kingdom. The second largest of the British Isles is called **Ireland.** Most of Ireland is an independent republic, but part of the north is governed as a province of the United Kingdom.

Great Britain has a landscape of rolling farmland. There are rugged highlands in Wales and Scotland, while England has rich farmland in the southeast, bleak moors in the north, flat fields in East Anglia and wild coasts in Cornwall. There are many beautiful old villages and towns, but also large cities and ports.

The Irish landscape is less crowded. It has green fields, misty hills and, in the west, steep cliffs pounded by Atlantic breakers. Its capital, Dublin, lies on the River Liffey.

English is spoken throughout the British Isles, but other languages may be heard too – Welsh, Irish and Scots Gaelic, and the various languages spoken by British people of Asian and African descent.

Both the UK and the **Republic of Ireland** are members of the

Wren

One of the most widespread birds of Britain, this short drab coloured bird with a cocked tail, has a loud warbling song. Wrens feed on caterpillars, beetles and bugs.

Highland games

Scottish pipers parade in the Highland Games. This competition has been taking place since the early nineteenth century, but has its roots

NORTH SEA

SHETLAND ISLANDS
Unst
Yell
Foula
Lerwick
Sumburgh Head
Fair Isle

SCOTLAND

Westray
ORKNEY ISLANDS
Kirkwall
Hoy
South Ronaldsay
John o'Groats
Thurso

Cape Wrath

Butt of Lewis
Stornoway
Lewis
North Minch

OUTER HEBRIDES
North Uist
South Uist
Barra

Skye
Rhum
Coll
Tiree
Mull
INNER HEBRIDES
Jura
Islay

Fraserburgh
Peterhead
Aberdeen
Dee
Montrose
SIDLAW HILLS
Dundee
Firth of Forth
Don
Spey
Moray Firth
Inverness
Loch Ness
NORTH WEST HIGHLANDS
GRAMPIAN MTS
Tay
Perth
OCHIL HILLS
Forth
Edinburgh
St. Abbs Head
Berwick-upon-Tweed
Tweed
Jedburgh
Mallaig
Ben Nevis ▲
1,343 m
Oban
Loch Lomond
Glasgow
Greenock
Clyde
Kilmarnock
Arran
Ayr
Kintyre Pen.

SCOTLAND

Tory I.
Malin Head
NORTHERN IRELAND
Holy I.
Rathlin I.

ENGLAND
UNITED KINGDOM

OCEAN

Erris Head

Achill Head

Donegal Bay

Clew Bay

Lough Conn

Lough Mask

Lough Corrib

Galway Bay

Galway

REPUBLIC OF IRELAND

ARAN ISLANDS

Loop Head

Bantry Bay

Dingle Bay

Gt. Blasket I.

Mizen Head

Kenmare River

Carrauntoohill 1,041 m

Killarney

Bantry

Cork

Limerick

Blackwater

GALTY MTS.

Tipperary

Lough Derg

Shannon

Athlone

Lough Ree

Lough Allen

Sligo

Donegal

DONEGAL MTS.

Lower Lough Erne

Upper Lough Erne

Armagh

NORTHERN IRELAND

ANTRIM MTS.

Lough Neagh

Belfast

Slieve Donard 852 m

Dundalk

Boyne

BOG OF ALLEN

Liffey

Dublin

Dun Laoghaire

WICKLOW MTS.

IRELAND

Nore

Barrow

Carlow

Waterford

Wexford

Hook Head

Old Head of Kinsale

Wicklow Head

Stranraer

Carlisle

Solway Firth

Durham

Middlesbrough

Scarborough

Flamborough Head

Spurn Head

Kingston upon Hull

NORTH YORK MOORS

Swale

York

Leeds

Bradford

Oldham

Manchester

Preston

Blackpool

Lake District

Scafell Pike 978 m

PENNINES

Morecambe Bay

Walney I.

Isle of Man

Douglas

IRISH SEA

Anglesey

Holyhead

Llandudno

Caernarfon Bay

Snowdon 1,085 m

CAMBRIAN MTS.

Cardigan Bay

Aberystwyth

Bardsey I.

WALES

Cardigan

Carmarthen

St. Brides Bay

Milford Haven

Gower Peninsula

Swansea

Newport

Cardiff

Bristol Channel

Wigan

Liverpool

Wrexham

Stoke on Trent

Wolverhampton

Walsall

Birmingham

Coventry

Severn

Wye

Cheltenham

Gloucester

Bristol

MENDIP HILLS

Bridgwater

Ilfracombe

EXMOOR

Lundy

Bude

DARTMOOR

Exeter

Bournemouth

Torbay

Portland Bill

Lyme Bay

Plymouth

St. Ives

Penzance

Lands End

Lizard Point

ISLES OF SCILLY

Nottingham

Derby

Leicester

Rotherham

Sheffield

Welland

Peterborough

THE FENS

The Wash

Norwich

EAST ANGLIA

Cambridge

Ipswich

Colchester

Chelmsford

Northampton

Milton Keynes

Luton

Oxford

CHILTERNS

Swindon

Reading

Basingstoke

Salisbury

HAMPSHIRE DOWNS

Winchester

Southampton

Portsmouth

Isle of Wight

LINCOLN WOLDS

Trent

ENGLAND

COTSWOLD HILLS

London

Thames

NORTH DOWNS

Canterbury

Dover

Folkestone

THE WEALD

SOUTH DOWNS

Hastings

Brighton

Southend-on-Sea

Alderney,

CHANNEL ISLANDS

Guernsey

Jersey

ENGLISH CHANNEL

N

Tower of London

Built in the eleventh century by William the Conqueror, this ancient fortress on the river Thames was once a royal home. It is now a museum and houses the crown jewels. It was here that Anne Boleyn, wife of Henry VIII, was beheaded. Yeomen of the Guard, or Beefeaters, still guard the Tower.

Ladies' View, Killarney, Eire

This famous beauty spot in southern Ireland enjoys wonderful views of Macgillycuddyís Reeks (a mountain range) and the lakes of Killarney. Of these lakes Lough Learne, or lower lake, is the largest with over 30 islands.

13

FRANCE AND MONACO

FRANCE IS A LARGE, beautiful country which lies at the heart of Western Europe. Its western regions include the massive peaks of the Pyrenees, vineyards and pine forests, peaceful rivers and Atlantic shores.

The north includes the stormy headlands of Brittany, the cliffs of Normandy and the Channel ports. Rolling fertile plains are drained by the winding river Seine, over whose banks and islands sprawls the French capital. Paris is one of the world's great cities, with broad avenues, historic palaces and churches.

The west of **France** is bordered by wooded hills which rise to the high forested slopes of the Jura mountains and finally the spectacular glaciers and ridges of the Alps. The rocks of the Massif Central, shaped by ancient volcanoes, rise in central southern France, to the west of the Rhône valley. The sun-baked hills of southern France border the warm seas of the Mediterranean Sea. This coast includes the wetlands of the Camargue, the great seaport of Marseilles and the fashionable yachting marinas of Cannes.

France has played a major part in history, and the French language is now spoken in many parts of the world. The French people are mostly descended from a Celtic people called the Gauls and Germanic peoples, such as the Franks and Vikings. Within France are several other peoples with their own languages and distinct cultures, such as Bretons, Basques, Catalans, Alsatians, Corsicans and Algerians.

France is a republic belonging to the European Union (EU) and is an important industrial power, producing cars, aerospace equipment, chemicals and textiles. The country is renowned for its wines, its cheeses, and its fine cooking.

Part of the Mediterranean coast is occupied by a very small principality called **Monaco**. It has close links with its large neighbour and shares the same currency. The state is famous for its casino.

Château de Charumont
France has many historical castles, palaces and stately homes, or châteaux. Some of the finest are in the Loire valley.

Cherbour
Carenta
S.
Gulf of St-Malo Gran
• Morlaix St.-Malo
• Brest St-Brieuc • Dinan
Fouge
• Douernenez
• Quimper • Pontivy Rennes
Lorient
• Vannes
• Redon
St. Nazaire
Belle-Ile
Nantes
La Roche-sur-
Isle d'Yeu
Les Sables-d'Olor

Cape Corse

• Bastia

CORSICA

Gulf of Sagone • Ajaccio

Bonifacio

Strait of Bonifacio

Ré I.
La Roche
Roche
Oléron
Ro

Pau

Sacré-Coeur
The gleaming domes of this church soar above the Parisian district of Montmartre, once famed as the haunt of artists and writers.

Bayon

Biarritz

P

S P A

Shape of the future
The Futuroscope theme park and study centre, near Poitiers, is one example of France's many experimental modern buildings. This theatre looks like a huge crystal.

Vineyard harvest
Grapes are gathered at a vineyard in Alsace, on the slopes of the Vosges. Grapes, grown in many regions of France, are made into some of the world's finest wines.

14

Dunkerque
Calais
Boulogne
Lille
Montreuil
Arras
Douai
Valenciennes
Abbeville
Cambrai
Dieppe
St. Quentin
Hirson
Fécamp
Amiens
Charleville-Mézières
Bolbec
Montdidier

BELGIUM
LUXEMBOURG

Bay of
the Seine
Le Havre
Rouen
Beauvais
Compiègne
Reims
Verdun
Metz

Caen
Louviers
Seine
Meaux
Marne
Pont à Mousson

GERMANY

Lisieux
Evreux
Paris
Châlons-sur-Marne
Nancy
Strasbourg

Argentan
St. Germain-en-Laye
Versailles
St.Dizier
Toul

NORMANDY HILLS
Alençon
Rambouillet
Fontainebleau
Seine
Moselle
Epinal
Colmar

Mayenne
Chartres
Nemours
Troyes
Saône
Mulhouse

Laval
Orléans
Sens
Langres
LANGRES PLATEAU
Montbéliard

VOSGES
Rhine

Le Mans
Montargis
Auxerre

Loire
Blois
Gien
Avallon
Dijon
Besançon

Angers
Tours
Doubs

Saumur
Vierzon
Loire
Dôle

Châtellerault
Bourges
Nevers
Autun
Chalon-sur-Saône

Cher
Châteauroux
Le Creusot

Poitiers
La Châtre
Moulins
Montceau les Mines
St.Claude

Niort
Montluçon
Mâcon
Bourg-en-Bresse

Civray
F R A N C E
Vichy
Villefranches
Annecy

Cognac
Limoges
Lyon
Villeurbanne
Chamonix
Mont Blanc
4,807m

Angoulême
Clermont-Ferrand
St.-Étienne
Chambéry

Nontron
Puy de Sancy
1,886m
Vienne
Val d'Isère

Barbezieux
MASSIF
CENTRAL
Annonay

Périgueux
Grenoble

Libourne
Aurillac
Romans-sur-Isère

Bergerac
Souillac
Valence

Bordeaux
Dordogne
Cère
Prives
Drac

Marmande
Lot
Lot
Montélimar
Gap

Cahors
Rodez
Mende
Durance

LES LANDES
Agen
Aveyron
Alès
Verdon

Garonne
Millau

Monte-de-Marsan
Montauban
Tarn
Avignon
Carpentras

Gaillac
Albi
CÉVENNES
Nîmes
Durance

Auch
Toulouse
Arles
Aix-en-Provence
Nice
MONACO

Tarbes
Castres
Montpellier
Cannes

Lourdes
Garonne
Carcassonne
Béziers
Sète
St.Raphael

St. Gaudens
Ariège
Narbonne
Marseille
Brignoles
St.Tropez
Côte d'Azur

PYRENEES
Aude
Toulon

Foix
Perpignan

ANDORRA

SWITZERLAND

ALPS

ITALY

FRANCE

MONACO

N

Quiche Lorraine
A speciality of north-eastern
France, this is a baked pastry
tart filled with eggs, cream,
cheese and bacon.

15

NORTH SEA
BALTIC SEA

Sylt
Flensburg
Schleswig
Kiel Bay
Kiel
Neumünster
Fehmarn
Rügen
Stralsund
Mecklenburg Bay
Rostock
Wismar
Güstrow
Schwerin
Neubrandenburg
Helgoland
Rendsburg
Cuxhaven
Itzehoe
Lübeck
Elmshorn
Norderstedt
Bremerhaven
Hamburg
Wilhelmshaven
Emden
Buxtehude
Müritz Lake
Neustrelitz
Papenburg
Oldenburg
Bremen
Lüneburg
Delmenhorst
Weser
Uelzen
Elbe
Wittenberge
Eberswalde-Finow
Oder
Nordhorn
Vechta
Nienburg
Celle
Stendal
Brandenburg
Berlin
POLAND
Rheine
Osnabrück
Weser
Hannover
Aller
Wolfsburg
Potsdam
Frankfurt (an der Oder)
Gronau
Minden
Hildesheim
Brunswick (Braunschweig)
Magdeburg
Eisenhüttenstadt
TEUTOBURG FOREST
Bielefeld
Hameln
Salzgitter
Neisse
Münster
Holzminden
Bad Harzburg
Halberstadt
Dessau
Cottbus
Bocholt
Hamm
Paderborn
Leine
Göttingen
HARZ MTS.
Halle
Hoyerswerda
Dinslaken
Dortmund
Münden
Nordhausen
Leipzig
Meissen
Duisburg
Essen
Arnsberg
Kassel
GERMANY
Görlitz
Krefeld
Wuppertal
Mönchen-Gladbach
Remscheid
Mühlhausen
Weimar
Dresden
Freiberg
Düsseldorf
Solingen
Erfurt
Jena
Gera
Chemnitz
Cologne (Köln)
Bergisch-Gladbach
Marburg
Zwickau
Aachen
Bonn
Siegen
Alsfeld
THURINGIAN FOREST
Plauen
Neuwied
Giessen
Fulda
Fulda
Werra
Suhl
Hof
CZECH REPUBLIC
Daun
Koblenz
Main
Coburg
Wiesbaden
Frankfurt am Main
Schweinfurt
Bayreuth
Mosel
Rhine
Mainz
Offenbach
Würzburg
Bamberg
Trier
Darmstadt
Main
Kitzingen
HUNSRÜCK
Worms
Mannheim
STEIGERWALD
Fürth
Nuremberg (Nürnberg)
BOHEMIAN FOREST
Saar
Ludwigshafen
Jagst
Kaiserslautern
Heidelberg
Saarbrücken
Karlsruhe
Heilbronn
Regensburg
Pforzheim
Stuttgart
Aalen
Ingolstadt
Passau
Baden-Baden
Tübingen
Danube
Baden-Baden
Neckar
Reutlingen
Ulm
Augsburg
Linz
SWABIAN JURA
Inn
Braunau
Rhine
BLACK FOREST
Munich (München)
Wels
Steyr
Freiburg
Memmingen
Lech
Rosenheim
Gmunden
Salzach
Salzburg
Schaffhausen
Konstanz
Kempten
Hallein
Winterthur
Lake Constance (Bodensee)
Kufstein
AUSTRIA
Basel
Baden
St Gallen
Kitzbühel
Solothurn
Zurich
LIECHTENSTEIN
Vaduz
Zugspitze 2,963 m
NIEDERE TAUERN
Neuchâtel
Lucerne
Zug
Innsbruck
Mur
Bern
Brenner
HOHE TAUERN
Lake Neuchâtel
Fribourg
SWITZERLAND
Chur
Davos
Grossglockner 2,863 m
Wolfsbe
Lausanne
Thun
Interlaken
Andermatt
Villach
Klagenfur
Lake Geneva
Montreux
St Moritz
ITALY
Drav
Thonon
BERNESE ALPS
LEPONTINE ALPS
SLOVENI
Geneva
Zermatt
Locarno
Bellinzona
Matterhorn 4,478 m
Monte Rosa 4,634 m
Lugano
JURA

N

SWITZERLAND

BELGIUM
LUXEMBOURG
FRANCE

GERMANY

LIECHTENSTEIN

AUSTRIA

GERMANY & THE ALPS

GERMANY LIES BETWEEN Western and Central Europe. In the south the high peaks of the Alps are flanked by belts of forest.

The rolling hills and heathland of the centre stretch to the North Sea, while in the west the rivers Rhine and Moselle wind through steep valleys planted with vines. In the northeast a vast plain is bordered by the Baltic Sea and by the rivers Oder and Neisse.

For most of its history Germany has been divided into different states. Today's united Germany dates from 1990. Germany is a federal republic, which means that its regions or Länder have considerable powers. The country is a leading member of the European Union and is a major world producer of cars, electrical and household goods, medicines, chemicals, wines and beers.

Switzerland is a small country set amongst the lakes and snowy peaks of the Alps and the Jura ranges. Its beautiful landscape and historical towns attract many tourists. Industries include dairy produce, precision instruments and finance. Zurich is a world centre of banking, while Geneva is the headquarters of many international agencies, such as the Red Cross and the World Health Organization.

To the east, the tiny country of **Liechtenstein** is closely linked with Switzerland and uses the same currency. The land of **Austria** descends from the soaring peaks of the Alps to the flat lands of the Danube river valley. Austria once ruled a large empire which stretched eastwards into Hungary and southwards into Italy. Today Austria still plays an important part in Europe, making its living from tourism, farming, forestry and manufacture.

German is spoken through most of the region, with a great variety of dialects. In parts of Switzerland there are people who speak French, Italian and Romansh.

Edelweiss
This small herb, with its pretty white flower, grows in the European Alps. High mountain meadows are filled with wildflowers in spring and summer.

Brimming with beer
Munich, capital of Bavaria in southern Germany, hosts a famous beer festival every October. Regional dress is still common in the region.

River of ice
This impressive glacier grinds its way down the Alps near Zermatt. Many tourists and climbers visit Switzerland to enjoy the spectacular views.

Medieval revelry
Festival costumes recall the Middle Ages in Baden Württemberg. During that period Germany was made up of many small states.

Krems
Danube
Vienna
t Pölten
Bruck
Baden
Neusiedler
Wiener Neustadt
See
apfenberg
en
Graz
HUNGARY

IBERIAN PENINSULA

THE IBERIAN PENINSULA is in southwestern Europe, and juts out into the Atlantic Ocean. It is bordered to the north by the stormy Bay of Biscay and to the south by the Mediterranean Sea and the Balearic Islands. Across the Strait of Gibraltar, just 13 kilometres away, lies the continent of Africa.

The north coast, green from high rainfall, rises to the Cantabrian mountains, while the snowy Pyrenees form a high barrier along the Spanish-French frontier. Another range, the Sierra Nevada, runs parallel with the south coast. Inland, much of the Iberian peninsula is taken up by an extremely dry, rocky plateau, which swelters in the heat of summer. To the west are forested highlands and the fertile plains of Portugal, crossed by great rivers such as the Douro, Tagus and Guadiana.

The Iberian peninsula is occupied by four countries or territories. There is **Gibraltar**, a British colony since 1713, and the tiny independent state of **Andorra**, high in the Pyrenees. The two main countries of the region are **Spain** and **Portugal**. Both have a history of overseas settlement, and both Spanish and Portuguese have become the chief languages of Latin America. Many people speak other languages, including Basque and Catalan, and have their own traditions and history.

Both Spain and Portugal were ruled by dictators for much of the 20th century, but today both are democracies and members of the European Union. Spain produces olives, citrus fruits, wines and sherries, and has a large fishing fleet. Portugal also produces wine and port takes its name from the city of Oporto. Fishing villages line the coasts and cork, used for bottle stoppers and tiling, is cut from the thick bark of the cork oak tree.

PORTUGAL

Feria in Seville
At the Feria, held in the Spanish city of Seville every April, people ride into town dressed in traditional finery. The river is lined with tents and pavilions. The festival is celebrated with bullfights, flamenco music and dancing.

Map labels

Bay of Biscay
Cape Ortegal
Cape Peñas
La Coruña
El Ferrol
Gijón
Villalba
Oviedo
Llan
Carballo
Fonsagrada
CANTABRIA
Cape Finisterre
Lugo
Sil
Santiago de Compostela
Sarria
Lalin
Monforte de Lemos
León
Astorga
Miño
Orense
SIERRA CABRERA
Vigo
La Gudina
Villada
Baltar
Esla
Braga
Bragança
Vallado
Tâmega
Tuela
Mogadouro
Zamora
Vila Real
Medina del Campo
Porto
Douro
Tormes
Lamego
Salamanca
PORTUGAL
Aviero
Viseu
Cuidad Rodrigo
Guarda
Béjar
Coimbra
Covilhã
SIERRA DE GREDOS
Castelo Branco
Plasencia
Tajo
Leiria
Tomar
Cáceres
Trujillo
Caldas da Rainha
Tagus
Santarém
Portalegre
Lisbon
Badajoz
Don Benito
Setúbal
Évora
Almendralejo
Pozoblanco
Ardila
Azuaga
Beja
Guadiana
SIER
Constantina
Córd
Chança
Nerva
Guadalquivir
Huelva
Seville
Puente Ge
Osuna
Lagos
Las Marismas
Faro
Costa de la Luz
Morón de la Fronte
Cape Saint Vincent
Algarve
Gulf of Cadiz
Ronda
Jerez de la Frontera
SIERRA DE RONDA
Cádiz
Marbe
Gibraltar (U.K
Algeciras
Strait of Gibralta
Cueta (Spair

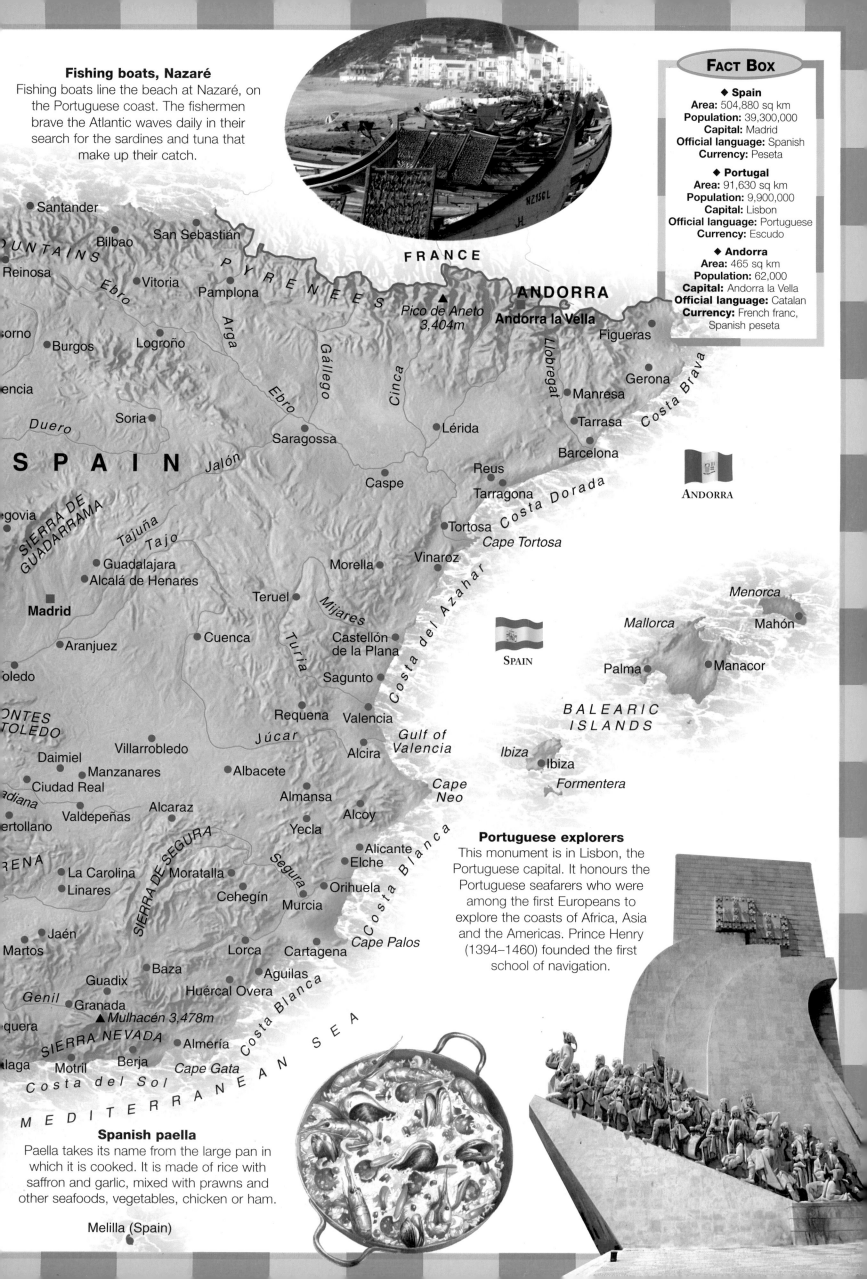

Fishing boats, Nazaré
Fishing boats line the beach at Nazaré, on the Portuguese coast. The fishermen brave the Atlantic waves daily in their search for the sardines and tuna that make up their catch.

FACT BOX

◆ **Spain**
Area: 504,880 sq km
Population: 39,300,000
Capital: Madrid
Official language: Spanish
Currency: Peseta

◆ **Portugal**
Area: 91,630 sq km
Population: 9,900,000
Capital: Lisbon
Official language: Portuguese
Currency: Escudo

◆ **Andorra**
Area: 465 sq km
Population: 62,000
Capital: Andorra la Vella
Official language: Catalan
Currency: French franc, Spanish peseta

Santander
Bilbao
San Sebastián
Reinosa
OUNTAINS
Ebro
Vitoria
Pamplona
PYRENEES
FRANCE
Pico de Aneto 3,404m
ANDORRA
Andorra la Vella
Figueras
orno
Burgos
Logroño
Arga
Gállego
Cinca
Llobregat
Gerona
Manresa
Costa Brava
encia
Duero
Soria
Ebro
Lérida
Tarrasa
SPAIN
Saragossa
Jalón
Barcelona
Caspe
Reus
Tarragona
Costa Dorada
govia
SIERRA DE GUADARRAMA
Tajuña
Tajo
Tortosa
Cape Tortosa
ANDORRA
Guadalajara
Alcalá de Henares
Morella
Vinaroz
Costa del Azahar
Madrid
Teruel
Mijares
Menorca
Aranjuez
Cuenca
Turia
Castellón de la Plana
Mallorca
Mahón
oledo
Sagunto
SPAIN
Palma
Manacor
ONTES TOLEDO
Requena
Valencia
BALEARIC ISLANDS
Villarrobledo
Júcar
Alcira
Gulf of Valencia
Daimiel
Albacete
Ibiza
Ibiza
Manzanares
Cape Neo
Formentera
Ciudad Real
Almansa
Alcoy
adiana
Valdepeñas
Alcaraz
Yecla
ertollano
Alicante
Elche
RENA
La Carolina
Moratalla
SIERRA DE SEGURA
Segura
Orihuela
Costa Blanca
Linares
Cehegín
Murcia
Jaén
Lorca
Cartagena
Cape Palos
Martos
Baza
Aguilas
Guadix
Huércal Overa
Genil
Granada
Costa Blanca
▲ Mulhacén 3,478m
quera
SIERRA NEVADA
Almería
MEDITERRANEAN SEA
alaga
Motril
Berja
Cape Gata
Costa del Sol

Portuguese explorers
This monument is in Lisbon, the Portuguese capital. It honours the Portuguese seafarers who were among the first Europeans to explore the coasts of Africa, Asia and the Americas. Prince Henry (1394–1460) founded the first school of navigation.

Spanish paella
Paella takes its name from the large pan in which it is cooked. It is made of rice with saffron and garlic, mixed with prawns and other seafoods, vegetables, chicken or ham.

Melilla (Spain)

ITALY AND ITS NEIGHBOURS

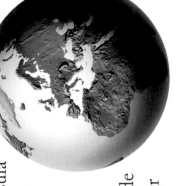

ITALY OCCUPIES a long, boot-shaped peninsula which stretches south from the snowy peaks and blue lakes of the Alps into the Mediterranean Sea. The country also takes in the large islands of Sardinia and Sicily. The northern regions of the mainland include the wide, fertile plains around the river Po and wealthy industrial cities.

A long chain of mountains, the Appenines, run down the spine of Italy. They descend to coastal farmland and the hot, dry plains of the south. Southern Italy and its islands are one of the world's volcanic danger zones. Olives and grapes grow well in its sunny climate and Italy is the largest wine producer in the world. Factories produce cars, textiles and leather goods.

Modern Italy has only been united since 1861, but in ancient times Rome was the capital of a vast empire which stretched across western Europe, southwest Asia and North Africa. Rome later became the centre of the Catholic Church and during the 1400s and 1500s cities such as Florence saw a great flowering of scholarship and the arts, known as the Renaissance. Many tourists visit Italy to see its ancient sites.

Italian, based on the ancient Latin language, is spoken throughout Italy, but in border regions you may hear other languages – French, German or Slovenian. The Ladin language is spoken in the Dolomite mountains and the people of Sardinia speak their own ancient dialect of Italian.

Two small independent states lie entirely surrounded by Italian territory. One is the world's smallest country, known as **Vatican City**. It is a district of Rome which serves as headquarters for the Pope and the Roman Catholic Church. The other is tiny **San Marino.**

South of Italy, towards the coast of North Africa is the chain of islands which make up **Malta**. The Maltese have their own language and live from building and repairing ships and from tourism.

Sun and sea

Portofino is a small town on the Gulf of Genoa, in Italy's Liguria region. Its pretty waterfront and fishing boats attract many tourists in the hot Mediterranean summer.

Spaghetti Bolognese

Spaghetti is a kind of pasta. Made from wheat and eggs, pasta is eaten in all kinds of shapes and sizes, each with its own name. Here it is served with a meat and tomato sauce, invented in the city of Bologna. Italians who have left their homeland have made their cooking popular around the world.

SLOVENIA

Trieste

Udine

Portogruaro

Bolzano

Borgo

Piave

Treviso

Venice

Chioggia

Trento

L. Garda

Vicenza

Padua

Adria

Comacchio

Verona

Mantova

Po

Ferrara

Ravenna

Rimini

AUSTRIA

Brescia

Oglio

Carpi

Panaro

Modena

Bologna

Forlì

Pesaro

San Marino

SAN MARINO

Ancona

Iesi

Macerata

San Benedetto

Bergamo

Cremona

Piacenza

Parma

Reggio nell'Emilia

Reno

Pistoia

Gubbio

Cortona

Perugia

Teramo

Lecco

Monza

Lodi

Pavia

A

Florence

Arezzo

Siena

L. Trasimeno

Milan

Como

Novi Ligure

Alessandra

La Spezia

Carrara

Massa

Lucca

Arno

Viareggio

Livorno

Pisa

Grosseto

Piombino

ITALY

SWITZERLAND

L. Maggiore

Ticino

Genoa

Savona

Gulf of Genoa

LIGURIAN SEA

VATICAN CITY

Biella

Monte Rosa 4,634m

Turin

Tanaro

Cuneo

MONACO

Mont Blanc 4,807m

Caprala

Elba

FRANCE

Italy

SAN MARINO

N
E
S
W

(France)

Vatican City
(in Rome)
Rome

Civitavecchia

Latina

Avezzano

Vasto

Termoli

Agnone

Isernia

Benevento

Naples

Salerno

▲Vesuvius 1,227m

Ischia

Capri

Gulf of Naples

Gulf of Gaeta

Foggia

Melfi

Potenza

L. Varano

Altamura

Bari

Brindisi

Taranto

Lecce

Gallipoli

Tricase

Gulf of Taranto

O f a n t o

Belvedere Marittimo

Rossano

Cosenza

Catanzaro

Crotone

Vibo Valentia

Reggio di Calabria

▲Mt. Etna 3,340m

Messina

Salina

Stromboli

Lipari

Vulcano

LIPARI ISLANDS

Palermo

S i c i l y

Catania

Gulf of Catania

Caltanissetta

Agrigento

Mazara del Vallo

Alcamo

Trapani

Cape San Vito

Gulf of Gela

Ragusa

Syracuse

Pantelleria

M A L T A   C H A N N E L

MALTA

MALTA

Strait of Bonifacio

Asinara

Gulf of Asinara

Alghero

Sassari

Olbia

Nuoro

Gulf of Orosei

S a r d i n i a

Tirso

Oristano

Cagliari

Gulf of Cagliari

San Pietro

The Leaning Tower

This famous marble bell tower was built in the Italian city of Pisa during the Middle Ages. Unfortunately, it was raised on unstable ground and soon began to sink. Today it leans over from the vertical by about 5 metres.

On the Gulf of Salerno

The seaport of Amalfi lies at the foot of Monte Cerreto, to the south-east of the city of Naples. The scenery here is spectacular.

Venice carnival

Elegant masks, cloaks and costumes in the style of the 1700s disguise revellers at Venice's famous carnival. Venice is one of the most beautiful cities in Europe.

CENTRAL EUROPE

THREE SMALL COUNTRIES cluster around the eastern shores of the Baltic Sea. **Estonia**, **Latvia** and **Lithuania** were part of the Soviet Union (today's Russian Federation) from 1940 until 1991, when they became independent. Their lands include forests and lakes, farmland and industrial cities.

Poland, which has historic links with Lithuania, is a large country which has also known invasions and foreign rule through much of its history. Despite this, the Poles, a Slavic people, have kept a sense of independence and a pride in their traditions. The lands near Poland's Baltic coast are dotted with lakes. The north is a flat land of pine forests, part of the great plain which stretches from eastern Germany into Russia. It is cold and snowy in winter, but warm in summer. In southern Poland the land rises to highlands and the jagged peaks of the Tatra mountains, along the Slovakian border.

Slovakia and the **Czech Republic** were a single country until 1993. Slovakia is a land of high mountains dropping to fertile farmland around the River Danube, which forms its southeastern border. When the two countries divided, most industry lay on the Czech side of the border. The Czech Republic produces beer, glass, ceramics, steel and machinery. The country is bordered by mountains and, in the east, by the Bohemian centre of learning and the arts.

The Czechs and Slovaks are both Slavic peoples, but the Hungarians are Magyars, a people who invaded and settled in the region about 1200 years ago. **Hungary** is a country of wide open plains and low mountains. Its fertile farmland produces fruits, grains and grapes for making strong red wine. Its beautiful capital Budapest is on the River Danube.

Historical Prague

Prague, capital of the Czech Republic, is a fine old city on the River Vltava. Prague was the chief city of independent Bohemia in the Middle Ages.

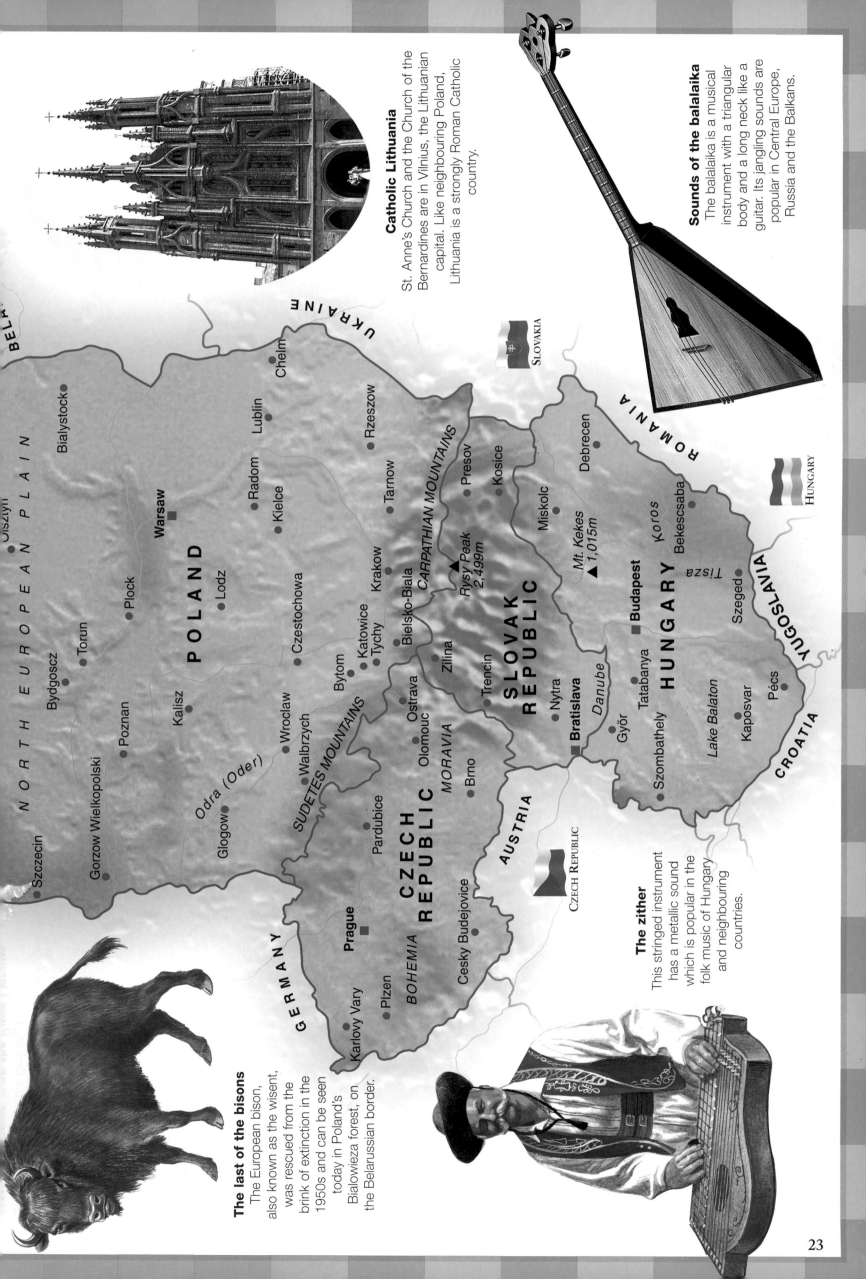

Catholic Lithuania

St. Anne's Church and the Church of the Bernardines are in Vilnius, the Lithuanian capital. Like neighbouring Poland, Lithuania is a strongly Roman Catholic country.

Sounds of the balalaika

The balalaika is a musical instrument with a triangular body and a long neck like a guitar. Its jangling sounds are popular in Central Europe, Russia and the Balkans.

The last of the bisons

The European bison, also known as the wisent, was rescued from the brink of extinction in the 1950s and can be seen today in Poland's Bialowieza forest, on the Belarussian border.

The zither

This stringed instrument has a metallic sound which is popular in the folk music of Hungary and neighbouring countries.

BELARUS

UKRAINE

SLOVAKIA

ROMANIA

HUNGARY

CZECH REPUBLIC

NORTH EUROPEAN PLAIN

Olsztyn

Bialystock

Szczecin

Gorzow Wielkopolski

Poznan

Bydgoscz

Torun

Plock

Kalisz

POLAND

Chelm

Lublin

Radom

Kielce

Warsaw

Lodz

Czestochowa

Rzeszow

Tarnow

Krakow

Bielsko-Biala

Katowice

Tychy

Bytom

Wroclaw

Walbrzych

Glogow

Odra (Oder)

SUDETES MOUNTAINS

Pardubice

Prague

BOHEMIA

CZECH REPUBLIC

Karlovy Vary

Plzen

Cesky Budejovice

Brno

MORAVIA

Olomouc

Ostrava

Zilina

Trencin

Presov

Kosice

CARPATHIAN MOUNTAINS

Rysy Peak ▲ 2,499m

SLOVAK REPUBLIC

Bratislava

Nytra

Miskolc

Debrecen

Mt. Kekes ▲ 1,015m

Budapest

HUNGARY

Györ

Tatabanya

Szombathely

Danube

Lake Balaton

Kaposvar

Szeged

Bekescsaba

Koros

Tisza

Pécs

AUSTRIA

GERMANY

YUGOSLAVIA

CROATIA

BALKANS AND ROMANIA

THE STATES OF SOUTHERN Central Europe are known as the Balkans. They take their name from the Balkan peninsula, a great wedge of land which stretches south into the Mediterranean.

SLOVENIA

CROATIA

BOSNIA-HERZEGOVINA

The warm, blue waters around the Balkan coast form the Adriatic, Aegean and Black Seas and are popular with tourists. The region is mountainous, with hot, dry summers. Winters are severe in the north of the region, but generally mild in the south. Earthquakes are common. The Balkan countries produce fruit, wines and spirits, dairy products such as yoghurt and cheese, olives, sunflowers and tobacco.

In the early 1990s the northwest of the region saw bitter fighting as the large nation of Yugoslavia broke up into separate independent states. These took the names of **Slovenia**, **Croatia**, **Bosnia-Herzegovina**, **Yugoslavia** (Serbia and Montenegro), and **Macedonia** (which is also the name of the northernmost province of Greece). The small and very poor country of **Albania** also suffered from political unrest and civil war in the 1990s.

The northeast of the Balkan peninsula is occupied by **Bulgaria**, a land of fertile farmland to the south of the river Danube, crossed by the Balkan and Rhodope mountain chains. Its northern neighbour is **Romania**, lying around the forested Carpathian mountain range and the Transylvanian Alps. On the Black Sea coast, the river Danube forms a marshy delta region.

The Balkan peninsula narrows to the south, breaking up into the headland of the Peloponnese and scattered island chains. **Greece** was the centre of Europe's first great civilizations, between 4,000 and 2,000 years ago. The rock of the Acropolis, with its temple, the Parthenon, still towers above the Greek capital, Athens.

Off to market
Romanian farmers gather for a cattle fair at Sugatag. The population as a whole is made up of Romanians, whose language is linked to the Latin language of the ancient Roman empire, as well as Magyars and Gypsies.

The sunflower crop
Sunflowers are grown in many parts of southern Europe. Their seeds may be roasted and eaten as snacks, turned into cooking oil or used to make margarine.

Old-fashioned style
Traditional Bulgarian costumes, with waistcoats, aprons and skirts may still be seen at many festivals or folk dances.

UKRAINE

Satu Mare

Baia Mare

Somes

Oradea   Cluj-Napoca   *Mures*

MOLDOVA

Botosani

Iasi

Tîrgu Mures

Bacau

Siret

ROMANIA

HUNGARY

Arad   *Mures*

Subotica

Timisoara

Alba Iulia

R O M A N I A

VOJVODINA

Deva   Sibiu   Brasov

Moldoveanu ▲
2,543 m

Galati

Braila

Resita

TRANSYLVANIAN ALPS

Novi Sad

Belgrade

cko

Sabac   Smederevo

Negotin

Jiu

Craiova

Ploiesti

Pitesti

Bucharest

DOBRUJA

Constanta

Valjevo   Kragujevac   Vidin

ebrenica   Cacac

Morava

Mikhaylovgrad

Iskur

Dunarea (Danube)

Ruse

Dobrich

Balchik

Novi Pazar   Krusevac   Nis

SERBIA

Leskovac

Sofia

Vratsa   Pleven

BALKAN MOUNTAINS

Lovech

Turgovishte

Shumen

Kamchiya

Varna

YUGOSLAVIA

NTENEGRO   Pristina

Kazanluk

Sliven

Burgas

Pec

KOSOVO

Pernik

BULGARIA

Tundzha Yambol

gorica

Lake Scutari

Urosevac

Musala Peak ▲
2,925 m

Pasardzhik

Maritsa

Stara Zagora

der

Mt Korabit ▲
2,751 m

Tetovo

Skopje

Plovdiv

Khaskovo

rin

ulf

Struma

PIRIN MTS

Smolyan

Orestiás

rrës

MACEDONIA

Vardar

Drama

RHODOPE MOUNTAINS

Komotini

Tiranë   Prilep

Palikastron

Xánthi

Elbasan   *Lake Ohrid*   Bitola

Sérrai

Kaválla

Alexandroúpolis

Lake Prespa   Edhessa

Kilkís

Thásos

ALBANIA   Náousa

Ptolemaís

Aliakmon

Thessaloníki

Samothrace

Vlore

Gjirokaster

Mt Olympus
▲ *2,917 m*

Mt Athos
▲ *2,033 m*

Límnos

Joánnina   Trikkala

Lárisa

G R E E C E

PINDUS MTS

Kérkira

Corfu   Párga

Vólos

Skíathos

Mitilíni

Arta

Kardhítsa

Skópelos   *Skíros*

Lesbos

Pálairos

Lamia

Euboea

A E G E A N

Leukas

Parnassus
▲ *2,547 m*

Kími

SEA

Astakós   Agrínion

Khalkís

Chios

Cephalonia

Ithaca

Pátrai

Mégara

Marathon

Ándros

Sámos

Athens

I O N I A N

Lambía   Corinth

Piraeus

Tínos

Ikaría

SEA

Amaliás

Argos

Kéa

Zante

Alfios

Láyrion

Míkonos

Pátmos

Pírgos

Návplion

Kíthnos

Síros

Páros

Léros

Trípolis

Galatás

Sérifos

Náxos

Kálimnos

P E L O P O N N E S U S

Sífnos

Ios

Cos

Kalamáta

Sparta

Mílos

Astipálaia

Tílos

Rhodes

Areópolis

Thíra

Rhodes Líndos

Neápolis

Cythera

SEA OF CRETE

Kárpathos

Khaniá

Iráklion

Réthimnon

Crete

Mt. Ida ▲
2,456 m

Islands from volcanoes

The Greek island of Santorini (or Thira) is one of the islands that form the Cyclades in the Aegean Sea. Once a volcano, the island has steep cliffs and narrow, winding streets. It has become a popular destination for tourists.

ROMANIA

YUGOSLAVIA

BULGARIA

MACEDONIA

GREECE

ALBANIA

FACT BOX

◆ **Slovenia**
Area: 20,250 sq km
Population: 1,990,000
Capital: Ljublana
Official language: Slovenian
Currency: Tolar

◆ **Croatia**
Area: 56,540 sq km
Population: 4,789,000
Capital: Zagreb
Official language:
Serbo-Croat
Currency: Croatian dinar

◆ **Bosnia-Herzegovina**
Area: 51,130 sq km
Population: 4,366,000
Capital: Sarajevo
Official language:
Serbo-Croat
Currency: Bosnian dinar

◆ **Yugoslavia (Serbia-Montenegro)**
Area: 102,170 sq km
Population: 10,600,000
Capital: Belgrade
Official language:
Serbo-Croat
Currency: Dinar

◆ **Macedonian (former Yugoslav) Republic**
Area: 25,715 sq km
Population: 2,173,000
Capital: Skopje
Official language:
Macedonian
Currency: Dinar

◆ **Albania**
Area: 28,750 sq km
Population: 3,363,000
Capital: Tiranë
Official language: Albanian
Currency: Lek

◆ **Romania**
Area: 237,500 sq km
Population: 22,767,000
Capital: Bucharest
Official language: Romanian
Currency: Leu

◆ **Bulgaria**
Area: 110,900 sq km
Population: 8,469,000
Capital: Sofia
Official language: Bulgarian
Currency: Lev

◆ **Greece**
Area: 131,985 sq km
Population: 10,500,000
Capital: Athens
Official language: Greek
Currency: Drachma

Clear waters
A waterfall sparkles in the sunshine in Croatia. This is a small country of many landscapes.

RUSSIA AND ITS NEIGHBOURS

FOR A LARGE PART OF THIS CENTURY all the countries on this map were part of one huge country, the Soviet Union. That nation was formed in the years after November 1917, when communists seized power from the czars. Communist rule ended in 1991 and many of the regions around the former Soviet borders then broke away to become independent countries.

St Basil's Cathedral, Russia
Moscow is famous for the onion-shaped domes of St Basil's Cathedral. It was built in 1555 by Czar Ivan IV to commemorate the defeat of invading Tartars.

The remaining part of the former Soviet Union was renamed the '**Russian Federation**'. It is still by far the largest country in the world, stretching across two continents, Europe and Asia. Eighty percent of the population are Russians, but the rest belong to one of the many other ethnic groups who live in this enormous region.

Northern Russia is a land of tundra, where deep-frozen soil borders the Arctic Ocean. To the south is the great belt of forest known as taiga, whose spruce trees are heavy with snow during the long, bitter winter. Southern Russia and the **Ukraine** have the fertile black earth of the rolling grasslands known as steppes. The lands to the south of Russia's new borders take in warm, fertile valleys, thin grasslands grazed by sheep and goats, deserts and high mountains.

Russia is rich in minerals, oil, natural gas and timber. Its industries were developed in a hurry during the Soviet years, but at great cost to its people and environment. Russia is still an economic giant, producing machinery, textiles, chemicals and vehicles.

Franz Josef Land

BARENTS SEA
Murmansk
Novaya Zemlya
KARA SEA

FINLAND
Archangel
Dikso
Amderma

BELARUS

L. Ladoga
St Petersburg
L. Onega
N. Dvina
Pechora
Salekhard

ESTONIA
LITHUANIA
LATVIA
RUSSIA

UKRAINE
BELARUS
Minsk
Smolensk
Yaroslavl'
Kirov
Ob'
SIBERIAN LOWLAND

Gomel
Moscow
Volga
Khanty-Mansiysk

Chernobyl
UKRAINE Kiev
Nizhniy Novgorod
Kazan
Kama
Perm
Nizhniy Tagil
U
R
U
S

MOLDOVA
Chisinau
Dnepr
Voronezh
Ufa
Irtysh
Tobol'sk
Yekaterinburg
Ob'

Khar'kov
Syzran
Chelyabinsk
Tom

Odessa
Don
Saratov
Samara
Magnitogorsk
Omsk

Donetsk
Volga
Ural
Orsk
Novosibirsk

Sevastopol
Volgograd
Rostov-on-Don

BLACK SEA
Astrakhan
Ishim
Aqmola
Irtysh
SAY

Mt. Elbrus 5,642 m
Groznyy
Caspian Sea
K A Z A K H S T A N
Karaganda

Batumi
CAUCASUS MTS.
Semey

MOLDOVA
GEORGIA
Tbilisi
ARMENIA
Yerevan
AZERBAIJAN
AZER.
Aral Sea
Syr Dar'ya
Balkhash

TURKEY
GEORGIA
Baku
TURANIAN PLATEAU
Lake Balkhash
CHINA

ARMENIA
Nukus
Tashauz
Almaty

UZBEKISTAN
TURKMENISTAN
Ashgabat
UZBEKISTAN
Bukhara
Bishkek
KYRGYZSTAN

IRAN
Amu Darya
Tashkent
KYRGYZSTAN

AZERBAIJAN
TURKMENISTAN
Dushanbe
TAJIKISTAN
AFGHANISTAN
TAJIKSTAN

26

Coarse cotton
Cotton of a tough, coarse grade is grown in Uzbekistan. The country is a major world producer, but in this dry land the cotton crop needs a great deal of irrigation, and this has harmed the environment.

Happy Easter!
Many Russians are Christians belonging to the Eastern Orthodox Church. Traditionally, they exchanged beautifully decorated eggs as gifts at Easter.

RUSSIA

Wrangel I.

Severnaya Zemlya

New Siberian Islands

EAST SIBERIAN SEA

Anadyr'

LAPTEV SEA

Os. Lyakhovskiy

Delta of the Lena

Kolyma

KOLIMA MOUNTAINS

KAMCHATKA PENINSULA

Commander Is.

Nordvik

Indigirka

CHERSKIY RANGE

KOLYMA LOWLAND

CENTRAL SIBERIAN PLATEAU

VERKHOYANSK RANGE

Lena

Magadan

Petropavlovsk-Kamchatskiy

Lower Tunguska

Yakutsk

DZUGDZHUR

SEA OF OKHOTSK

Olekminsk

ALDAN MOUNTAINS

Sakhalin

Lensk

Lena

STANOVOY RANGE

Tatarskiy Proliv

Yuzhno-Sakhalinsk

ngara

YABLONOVVY MOUNTAINS

Amur

Khabarovsk

SIKHOTE ALIN'

Bratsk

Krasnoyarsk

Lake Baykal

CHINA

Irkutsk

enisey S.

Ulan-Ude

MONGOLIA

Vladivostok

KAZAKHSTAN

N

In the Caucasus
This woman wears a traditional costume of Dagostan, a part of the Russian Federation which lies between the Caucasus mountains and the Caspian Sea. About 30 different ethnic groups live in this region.

FACT BOX

◆ **Russia**
Area: 17,078,005 sq km
Population: 148,673,000
Capital: Moscow
Official language: Russian
Currency: Rouble

◆ **Belarus**
Area: 208,000 sq km
Population: 10,313,000
Capital: Minsk
Official language: Belarussian
Currency: Rouble

◆ **Ukraine**
Area: 603,700 sq km
Population: 52,194,000
Capital: Kiev
Official language:Ukrainian
Currency: Karbovanets

◆ **Moldova**
Area: 33,7000 sq km
Population: 4,356,000
Capital: Chisinau
Official language: Moldovan
Currency: Leu

◆ **Kazakhstan**
Area: 2,717,300 sq km
Population: 17,035,000
Capital: Almaty
Official language: Kazakh
Currency: Tenge

◆ **Armenia**
Area: 30,000 sq km
Population: 3,677,000
Capital: Yerevan
Official language: Armenian
Currencies: Dram, rouble

◆ **Georgia**
Area: 69,700 sq km
Population: 5,471,000
Capital: Tbilisi
Official language: Georgian
Currency: Lari

◆ **Azerbaijan**
Area: 87,000 sq km
Population: 7,398,000
Capital: Baku
Official language: Azeri
Currencies: Manat, rouble

◆ **Turkmenistan**
Area: 488,100 sq km
Population: 3,714,000
Capital: Ashkhabad
Official language: Turkmen
Currency: Manat

◆ **Uzbekistan**
Area: 447,400 sq km
Population: 21,207,000
Capital: Tashkent
Official language: Uzbek
Currencies: Som, rouble

◆ **Tajikstan**
Area: 143,100 sq km
Population: 5,514,000
Capital: Dushanbe
Official language: Tajik
Currency: Rouble

◆ **Kyrgyzstan**
Area: 198,500 sq km
Population: 4,528,000
Capital: Bishkek
Official language: Kyrgyz
Currency: Som

CANADA AND GREENLAND

CANADA is the second largest country in the world and yet it is home to only 30 million people. Most Canadians live in the big cities in the south, such as Toronto, Ottawa, Montréal and Vancouver.

The southern provinces take in the St Lawrence River and Seaway, the Great Lakes, the prairies along the United States border and the foggy coasts of the Atlantic and Pacific Oceans.

The severe climate makes it hard for people to live in the northern wilderness, which stretches into the **Arctic Circle**. Here, a broad belt of spruce forest gives way to bare, deep-frozen soil called tundra, and a maze of islands locked in ice.

Canada's wilderness includes rivers, lakes, coasts and forests. It is home to polar bears and seals, caribou, moose, beavers and loons. It also has valuable resources, providing timber, hydroelectric power and minerals, including oil. **Canada** is a wealthy country.

The first Canadians crossed into North America from Asia long ago, when the two continents were joined by land. They were the Native American peoples and they were followed by the Inuit people of the Arctic. Today these two groups make up only four percent of the population. About 40 percent of Canadians are descended from peoples of the British Isles, especially Scots. People of French descent make up 27 percent, and there are also many people of Eastern European and Asian descent.

Canada has two official languages, French and English. In recent years many people in the French-speaking province of Québec have campaigned to become separate from the rest of Canada.

Across the Davis Strait, **Greenland** (or Kallaalit Nunaat) is a self-governing territory of Denmark. Its peoples are descended from both Inuit and Scandinavians.

ARCTIC OCEAN

Melville Island

Banks Island

Prince of Wales Island

BEAUFORT SEA

Victoria Island

ALASKA (U.S.A.)

Dawson

Norman Wells

Great Bear Lake

MACKENZIE MOUNTAINS

Mackenzie

YUKON TERRITORY

▲ Mt. Logan 5,951 m

Whitehorse

NORTHWEST TERRITORIE

Liard

HORN MOUNTAINS

Yellowknife

Dubawnt Lake

Great Slave Lake

Fort Resolution

Fort Smith

ROCKY

BRITISH COLUMBIA

CARIBOU MOUNTAINS

Lake Athabasca

CANADA

Peace

Reindeer Lake

Chur

Nels

Prince Rupert

COAST MOUNTAINS

Prince George

Peace River

ALBERTA

QUEEN CHARLOTTE ISLANDS

Fraser

Edmonton

N. Saskatchewan

Red Deer

Prince Albert

Lake Winnip

MANITO

Kamloops

MOUNTAINS

Lake Winnipegosis

Saskatoon

Vancouver Island

Calgary

SASKATCHEWAN

Lake Manitoba

Vancouver

Medicine Hat

S. Saskatchewan

Regina

Winnipe

Victoria

UNITED STATES OF AMERICA

Wheat Harvest
Large combine harvesters cross the Canadian prairies. These are natural grasslands which are now largely given over to wheat and cattle production. They occupy parts of Manitoba, Saskatchewan and Alberta and stretch across the border into the northern United States.

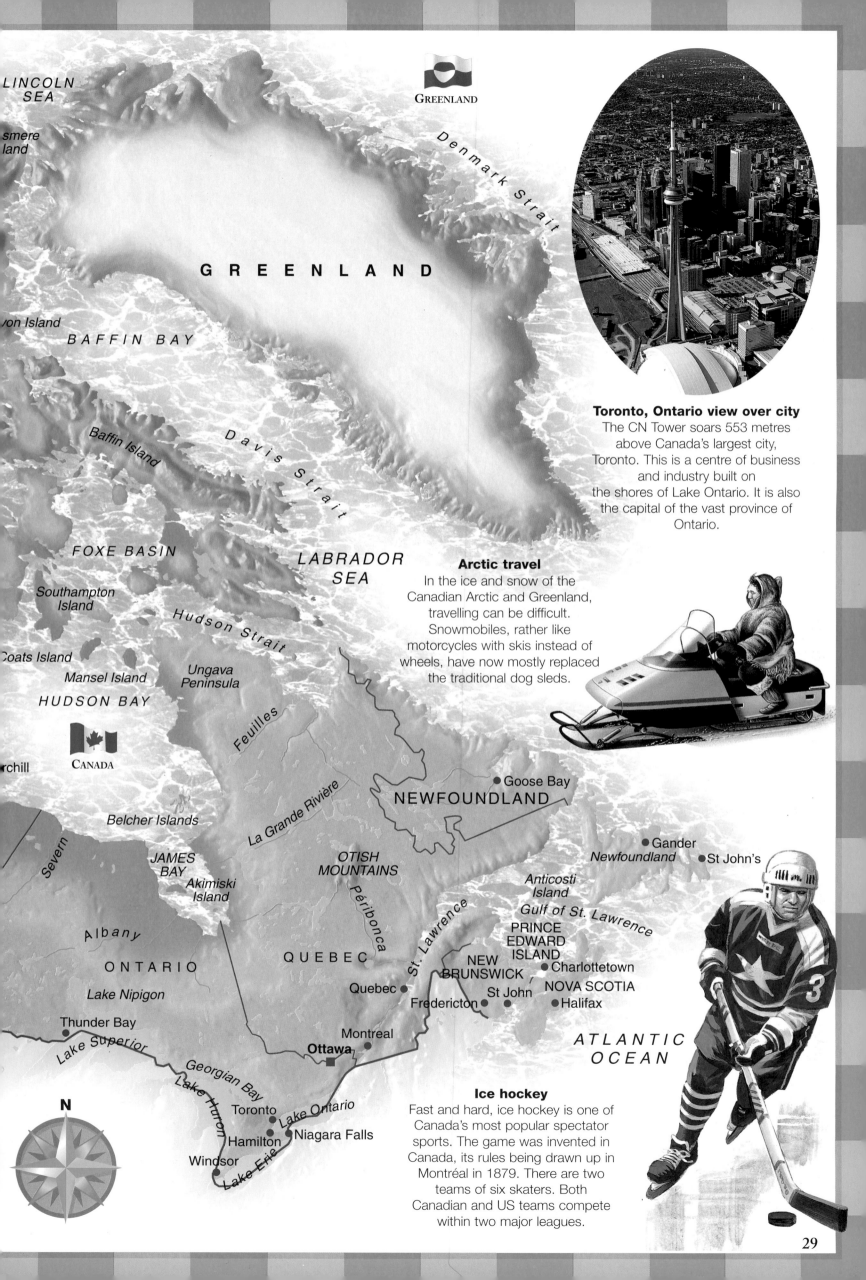

LINCOLN
SEA

GREENLAND

GREENLAND

Denmark Strait

smere
land

on Island

BAFFIN BAY

on Island

Baffin Island

Davis Strait

FOXE BASIN

LABRADOR
SEA

Southampton
Island

Hudson Strait

Coats Island

Mansel Island

Ungava
Peninsula

HUDSON BAY

CANADA

rchill

Feuilles

Goose Bay

NEWFOUNDLAND

La Grande Rivière

Belcher Islands

Gander

Newfoundland

St John's

Severn

JAMES
BAY

OTISH
MOUNTAINS

Akimiski
Island

Péribonca

Anticosti
Island

Gulf of St. Lawrence

St. Lawrence

PRINCE
EDWARD
ISLAND

Albany

ONTARIO

QUEBEC

NEW
BRUNSWICK

Charlottetown

Quebec

NOVA SCOTIA

Lake Nipigon

St John

Fredericton

Halifax

Thunder Bay

Montreal

ATLANTIC
OCEAN

Lake Superior

Ottawa

Georgian Bay

N

Lake Huron

Toronto

Lake Ontario

Hamilton

Niagara Falls

Windsor

Lake Erie

Toronto, Ontario view over city
The CN Tower soars 553 metres
above Canada's largest city,
Toronto. This is a centre of business
and industry built on
the shores of Lake Ontario. It is also
the capital of the vast province of
Ontario.

Arctic travel
In the ice and snow of the
Canadian Arctic and Greenland,
travelling can be difficult.
Snowmobiles, rather like
motorcycles with skis instead of
wheels, have now mostly replaced
the traditional dog sleds.

Ice hockey
Fast and hard, ice hockey is one of
Canada's most popular spectator
sports. The game was invented in
Canada, its rules being drawn up in
Montréal in 1879. There are two
teams of six skaters. Both
Canadian and US teams compete
within two major leagues.

USA

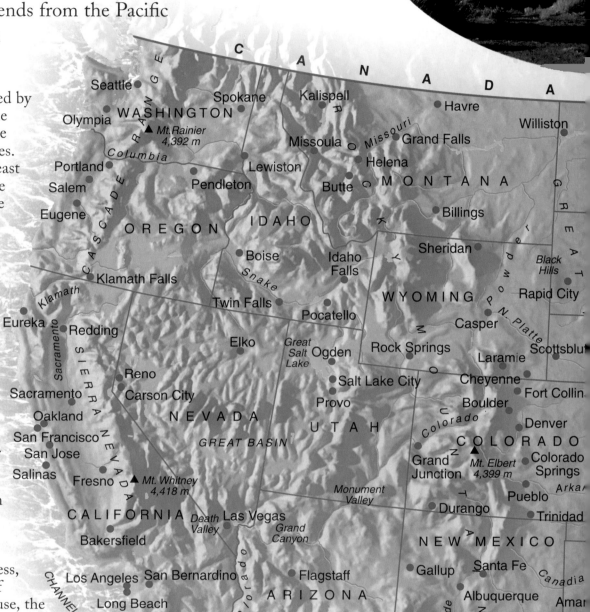

THE UNITED STATES OF AMERICA

make up a huge country, which crosses no less than eight time zones. It extends from the Pacific to the Atlantic Oceans, from Canada south to Mexico.

The modern nation was formed by colonists from Europe, who from the 1500s onwards seized and settled the lands of the Native American peoples. In 1776 the British colonies in the east declared their independence, and the new country grew rapidly during the 1800s as it gained territory from France, Mexico and Russia. Today, in addition to the small Native American population, there are Americans whose ancestors originally came from Britain, Ireland, Italy, France, Germany, the Netherlands and Poland. There are African Americans, whose ancestors were brought to America to work as slaves. There are Armenians, Spanish, Chinese, Cubans, Vietnamese and Koreans. All are citizens of the United States.

The nation today is a federation of 50 states, which have the power to pass many of their own laws. The federal capital is at Washington, a large city on the Potomac River, in the District of Columbia (DC). Here is the Congress, made up of a Senate and a House of Representatives, and the White House, the home of the US presidents.

The American economy is the most powerful in the world. The country is rich in minerals, including oil, coal and iron ore. American companies produce computers and software, aircraft, cars and processed foods. There are also many large banks and finance companies. America leads in space exploration and technology. The films and television programmes produced in America are watched by people in many countries around the world.

FACT BOX

◆ **United States of America**
   Area: 9,363,130 sq km
   Population: 267,700,000
   Capital: Washington DC
   Official language: English
   Currency: US dollar

The woods of Vermont

Vermont is in New England and nicknamed the Green Mountain State. It is famous for its brilliant foliage in the autumn or fall.

Monument Valley, Arizona
This spectacular landscape is sculpted by nature and is formed of red sandstone. There are many Wild West legends rooted here.

The Bald Eagle
This is America's national bird. It has a white head, and a wingspan of up to 2 metres. Its natural habitat is by lakes and rivers, and for food it preys mainly on fish and rodents.

THE UNITED STATES OF AMERICA

Lake Superior
Lake Huron
Lake Michigan
Lake Erie

MAINE
• Bangor
Augusta
Burlington
VERMONT
NEW HAMPSHIRE
Montpelier
Portland
Concord
NEW YORK
Rochester • Syracuse
Boston
MASSACHUSETTS
Cape Cod
Buffalo
Albany Hartford
Providence
RHODE ISLAND
CONNECTICUT
New York City
Scranton
NEW JERSEY
PENNSYLVANIA
Erie
Cleveland
Philadelphia
Trenton
Akron
Harrisburg
Dover
Pittsburgh
Baltimore
DELAWARE
Columbus
WASHINGTON D.C.
Annapolis
MARYLAND
OHIO
Dayton
WEST VIRGINIA
Chesapeake Bay
Cincinnati
Ohio
Charleston
Richmond
Frankfort
VIRGINIA
Norfolk
Louisville
Lexington
Roanoke

not
Grand Forks
MINNESOTA
ORTH
AKOTA
amestown
Duluth
Marquette
narck
Fargo
St. Cloud
WISCONSIN
Aberdeen
St Paul
Green Bay
Minneapolis
MICHIGAN
Grand Rapids
Detroit
rre
Sioux Falls
La Crosse
Milwaukee
Lansing
Windsor
OUTH
AKOTA
IOWA
Madison
Rockford
Toledo
Norfolk
Cedar Rapids
Chicago
Gary
Sioux City
Davenport
INDIANA
EBRASKA
Omaha
Des Moines
Peoria
Columbus
rand Island
ILLINOIS
Indianapolis
Platte
Lincoln
Springfield
Kansas City
Jefferson City
St. Louis
Evansville
MISSOURI
Abilene
Salina
Topeka
ANSAS
Hutchinson
Joplin
Paducah
KENTUCKY
Knoxville
Greensboro
Raleigh
Cape Hatteras
Wichita
Springfield
Nashville
Winston-Salem
NORTH CAROLINA
Cimarron
Tulsa
TENNESSEE
Charlotte
OKLAHOMA
ARKANSAS
Chattanooga
Greenville
Wilmington
Oklahoma City
Fort Smith
Memphis
SOUTH CAROLINA
Cape Fear
Arkansas
Tupelo
Tennessee
Alabama
Columbia
Little Rock
Birmingham
Atlanta
Augusta
Charleston
Wichita Falls
Texarkana
Greenville
Macon
Savannah
Dallas
Meridian
Columbus
ene
Brazos
Fort Worth
Shreveport
ALABAMA
GEORGIA
LOUISIANA
Jackson
Montgomery
TEXAS
Jackson
MISSISSIPPI
Albany
Waco
Alexandria
Mobile
Jacksonville
Angelo
Biloxi
Tallahassee
St. Augustine
Austin
Baton Rouge
Pensacola
Daytona Beach
Beaumont
Cape Canaveral
Houston
New Orleans
Orlando
San Antonio
Port Arthur
Tampa
FLORIDA
Galveston
Mississippi Delta
St. Petersburg
West Palm Beach
Fort Myers
Lake Okeechobee
Laredo
Corpus Christi
GULF OF MEXICO
Miami
Brownsville
Key West
Florida Keys
Straits of Florida

Red
Missouri
James
Mississippi
Red River
Ohio
Appalachian Mountains

N

The northeastern United States have a mild climate, although winter snowfall can be heavy and summers can be warm. Inland from the rocks and stormy shores of the Atlantic coast are the woodlands of the New England region, which turn to every shade of red and gold in the autumn. Here there are broad rivers and neat little towns dating back to the days of the early settlers, as well as the historic city of Boston, Massachusetts. In the far north the Great Lakes mark the border with Canada. On this border are the spectacular Niagara Falls, a major tourist attraction which also provides valuable hydroelectric power. The Appalachian mountain ranges run for 2,400 kilometres from north to south, through the eastern United States.

The northeastern United States include centres of industry and mining, and large cities with gleaming skyscrapers, sprawling suburbs, road and rail networks. New York City, centred around the island of Manhattan, is the business capital of the United States and also a lively centre of arts and entertainment. To many people, New York City is a symbol of America – fast-moving and energetic, a melting pot of different peoples and cultures. The northern city of Detroit is a centre of the motor industry, and Chicago, on the windy shores of Lake Michigan, is another bustling city of skyscrapers, and an important centre of business and manufacture.

Travelling south from the Delaware River and the great city of Philadelphia, you come to the federal District of Columbia, the site of Washington, capital city of the United States. Approaching the American South, you pass into warmer country where tobacco and cotton are grown in the red earth. The long peninsula of Florida extends southwards into the Caribbean Sea, fringed by sandy islands called keys. Along the Gulf coast the climate is hot and very humid, with creeks known as bayous and tangled swamps which are home to alligators.

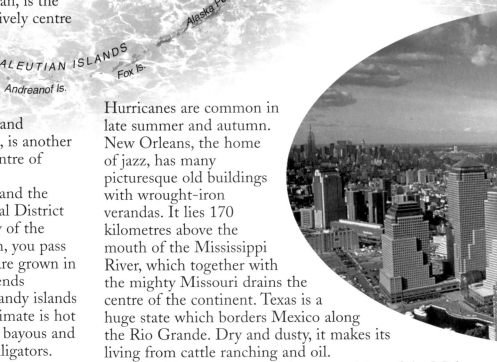

Hurricanes are common in late summer and autumn. New Orleans, the home of jazz, has many picturesque old buildings with wrought-iron verandas. It lies 170 kilometres above the mouth of the Mississippi River, which together with the mighty Missouri drains the centre of the continent. Texas is a huge state which borders Mexico along the Rio Grande. Dry and dusty, it makes its living from cattle ranching and oil.

Prairies once covered the great plains of the Midwest, the home of vast herds of bison or buffalo. Today the grasslands are largely given over to farming vegetable crops and grain, or to cattle ranching. The wheat and maize produced on the Prairies have led to them being called the 'breadbasket of the world'.

Barren, stony 'badlands' rise towards the rugged Rocky Mountain ranges, which form the backbone of the United States as they stretch from the Canadian border south to Mexico. Southwards and westwards again there are large areas of burning desert, salt flats and canyons, where over the ages the rocks have been worn into fantastic shapes by wind and water. In places the Grand Canyon of Arizona is 24 kilometres wide and two kilometres deep, a spectacular gorge cut out by the waters of the Colorado River.

Jambalaya!

Rice, seafood, green peppers and hot spices make up this delicious dish from New Orleans, in Louisiana. The people of this city include many of French and African descent, and this shows in its cooking.

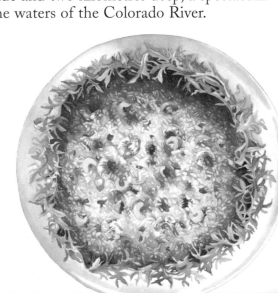

The Statue of Liberty

This huge monument, a gift from the people of France in 1886, was the first sight of America for many immigrants.

Badwater, in California's harsh Death Valley, is the lowest point in the United States, 86 metres below sea level.

The Sierra, Cascade and Coast ranges run parallel with the beautiful Pacific coast. The warm beaches, pines and gigantic redwood trees of California stretch northwards to the ferny forests of Oregon and Washington State, which is rainy and cool. Irrigation has made it possible to farm large areas of California, which produce citrus fruits and grape vines. Major cities of the west include Los Angeles, which takes in the world-famous film studios of Hollywood, beautiful San Francisco, set on a wide bay which can be warm and sparkling blue or shrouded in cool sea-fog, and the busy northern port of Seattle.

The United States has a northern outpost in oil-rich Alaska, its largest state. Alaska was purchased from Russia in 1867. Bordered by Canada, the Alaskan wilderness stretches into the remote Arctic, a deep frozen land of mountains and tundra.

Its islands are inhabited by large grizzly bears and its waters by schools of migrating whales.

Baseball
Baseball is the the big summer-season game in the USA. It is played with a bat and ball and there are two teams of nine players.

Mount McKinley, at 6,194 metres, is the highest point not just in the United States, but in all of North America.

Far to the west, in the Pacific Ocean, the Hawaiian Islands are also part of the United States. Tourists come here to enjoy the warm climate and the surf and to see the islands' spectacular volcanoes.

The United States also governs or has special links with various other territories, such as American Samoa, the Northern Marianas and the Midway Islands in the Pacific Ocean. Puerto Rico and the US Virgin Islands in the Caribbean are also governed by the United States.

The United States has close economic links with its neighbours, Canada and Mexico, through the North American Free Trade Agreement of 1994. It is also a member of many other international groupings, such as the the North Atlantic Treaty Organization (NATO), a military alliance which links it with Western and Central Europe.

As the world's most powerful country, the influence of the United States is to be seen in many other lands. Films and television programmes have made the American way of life influential around the world. Hamburgers and soft drinks are now bought in many other countries. American blues and jazz has influenced all kinds of popular music and American slang is used by people around the world.

Manhattan
The centre of New York City is built over the island of Manhattan. Unable to build outwards, architects have built upwards. The skyline includes many famous skyscrapers. These twin towers belong to the World Trade Centre.

Cops and crime
American policemen and detectives fight city crime. Their work has been made famous around the world by countless films and television series.

Heart of the nation
The impressive Capitol building is at the centre of Washington, District of Columbia. It is used by the United States Congress and was constructed between 1851 and 1863.

Blast-off!
The space shuttle leaves Earth on another mission. The United States has been a pioneer of space exploration since the 1960s.

MEXICO, CENTRAL AMERICA & THE CARIBBEAN

Ancient stones
Many great civilizations developed in ancient times in Mexico and Central America. Statues like this, called chacmools, were used during human sacrifices.

MEXICO is a large, mountainous country with a tropical climate. It stretches southwards from the Rio Grande on the United States border, and meets the Pacific Ocean in the west and the Gulf of Mexico in the east.

Mexico is a land of deserts, forests and volcanoes, dotted with the spectacular ruins of ancient Native American civilizations, such as the Maya, Toltec and Aztec. Mexico City, built on the site of an ancient Aztec city, is a vast, sprawling centre of population.

To the south, **Central America** narrows to a thin strip of land called the isthmus of Panama. Guatemala, Belize, Honduras, El Salvador, Nicaragua, Costa Rica and Panama are all small nations that live mostly by farming tropical crops such as bananas, coffee and sugar-cane. Many Mexicans and Central Americans are of Native American, Spanish or mixed descent.

Tijuana Mexicali
Ensenada
Cedros I.
Gulf of California
Baja California
La Paz
Cape Corrientes
Manzanillo

UNITED STATES OF AMERICA
Ciudad Juárez
Hermosillo
Chihuahua
SIERRA MADRE
Rio Bravo del Norte
Rio Grande
SIERRA MADRE
Torreón   Monterrey
Saltillo
Durango
San Luis Potosí
Aguascalientes
Guadalajara   León
L. de Chapala
MEXICO
Mexico City
Puebla   Veracruz
Orizaba
5,700 m
Balsas
Acapulco   Oaxaca

GULF OF MEXICO

Matamoros

MEXICO

Tampico

Mérida   Cancún
Yucatán Channel
Yucatán Peninsula
Bay of   Campeche
Campeche
Terminos
Lagoon
Villahermosa   Belize City
Belmopan
BELIZE
GUATEMALA   **HONDURAS**
Gulf of
Tehuantepec   Tegucigalpa
Guatemala City
San Salvador
EL SALVADOR   **NICARAGUA**
Lake
Nicaragua
Managua
Mosqu
Gul
San José
**COSTA
RICA**

Havana
CUBA   **CUBA**
Isla de la
Juventad
Caym
Islands (U
BELIZE

*PACIFIC
OCEAN*

N

EL SALVADOR   NICARAGUA

COSTA RICA

GUATEMALA

Birds of a feather
The quetzal is a brilliantly coloured bird. It lives in rainforests from southern Mexico to Panama, where it feeds on berries and fruits.

Many people in Mexico and Central America are poor and the region has a long history of political strife and civil war.

The **Caribbean Sea** is part of the Atlantic Ocean and is dotted with beautiful islands in warm, blue seas. These were once home to Native American peoples such as the Arawaks and the Caribs, after whom the region is named. Then came European invaders, including the Spanish, Dutch, French and British. Most of today's Caribbeans are descended from West Africans who were brought in as slaves by the early settlers. Caribbean islanders live by fishing, farming, manufacture and tourism. Favourite sports include baseball in Cuba and cricket in Jamaica and Barbados. The region is famous for its range of popular music, from calypso to salsa, from reggae to soca.

Coconut grove
Palms line sandy beaches in the Central American republic of Costa Rica. Coconuts are common around the tropical coasts of Central America and the Caribbean.

FACT BOX

◆ **Mexico**
Area: 1,972,545 sq km
Population: 95,700,000
Capital: Mexico City
Main language: Spanish
Currency: Mexican peso

◆ **Belize**
Area: 22,965 sq km
Population: 205,000
Capital: Belmopan
Main language: English
Currency: Belize dollar

◆ **Costa Rica**
Area: 50,900 sq km
Population: 3,500,000
Capital: San José
Main language: Spanish
Currency: Costa Rican colón

◆ **El Salvador**
Area: 21,395 sq km
Population: 5,900,000
Capital: San Salvador
Main language: Spanish
Currency: El Salvador colón

◆ **Guatemala**
Area: 108,890 sq km
Population: 11,200,000
Capital: Guatemala City
Main language: Spanish
Currency: Quetzal

◆ **Honduras**
Area: 112,085 sq km
Population: 5,800,000
Capital: Tegucigalpa
Main language: Spanish
Currency: Lempira

◆ **Nicaragua**
Area: 148,000 sq km
Population: 4,400,000
Capital: Managua
Main language: Spanish
Currency: Córdoba

◆ **Panama**
Area: 78,515 sq km
Population: 2,700,000
Capital: Panama City
Main language: Spanish
Currency: Balboa

◆ **Antigua and Barbuda**
Area: 442 sq km
Population: 100,000
Capital: St Johns
Main language: English
Currency: East Caribbean dollar

◆ **Bahamas**
Area: 13,865 sq km
Population: 300,000
Capital: Nassau
Main language: English
Currency: Bahamian dollar

◆ **Barbados**
Area: 430 sq km
Population: 300,000
Capital: Bridgetown
Main language: English
Currency: Barbados dollar

◆ **Cuba**
Area: 114,525 sq km
Population: 11,100,000
Capital: Havana
Main language: Spanish
Currency: Cuban peso

◆ **Dominica**
Area: 751 sq km
Population: 100,000
Capital: Roseau
Main language: English
Currency: East Caribbean dollar

◆ **Dominican Republic**
Area: 48,440 sq km
Population: 8,200,000
Capital: Santiago
Main language: Spanish
Currency: Peso

◆ **Grenada**
Area: 345 sq km
Population: 100,000
Capital: St George's
Main language: English
Currency: East Caribbean dollar

◆ **Haiti**
Area: 27,750 sq km
Population: 6,600,000
Capital: Port-au-Prince
Main language: French
Currency: Gourde

◆ **Jamaica**
Area: 11,425 sq km
Population: 2,600,000
Capital: Kingston
Main language: English
Currency: Jamaican dollar

◆ **St Christoper (St Kitts) – Nevis**
Area: 261 sq km
Population: 44,000
Capital: Basseterre
Main language: English
Currency: East Caribbean dollar

◆ **St Lucia**
Area: 616 sq km
Population: 139,000
Capital: Castries
Main language: English
Currency: East Caribbean dollar

◆ **St Vincent and the Grenadines**
Area: 389 sq km
Population: 111,000
Capital: Kingstown
Main language: English
Currency: East Caribbean dollar

◆ **Trinidad and Tobago**
Area: 5,130 sq km
Population: 1,300,000
Capital: Port of Spain
Main language: English
Currency: Trinidad & Tobago dollar

BAHAMAS
BAHAMAS

Turks & Caicos Islands (U.K.)

PUERTO RICO

Virgin Is. (U.K. & U.S.)

San Juan
Puerto Rico (U.S.)

DOMINICA

ANTIGUA & BARBUDA

Montserrat (U.K.)

Guadeloupe (FR.)

DOMINICA

Martinique (FR.)

ST. LUCIA

BARBADOS

ST. VINCENT & THE GRENADINES

GRENADA

TRINIDAD & TOBAGO

ANTIGUA AND BARBUDA

assau
ros I.

amagüey

ntiago
Cuba

DOMINICAN REPUBLIC

HAITI

Santo Domingo
Port-au-Prince

GREATER ANTILLES

Kingston

JAMAICA
CARIBBEAN SEA

LESSER ANTILLES

DOMINICAN REPUBLIC

JAMAICA

HAITI

Netherlands Antilles

HONDURAS

ST VINCENT AND GRENADINES

GRENADA

PANAMA
NAMA

COLOMBIA

ama ity
f of ama

TRINIDAD AND TOBAGO   ST LUCIA   BARBADOS   ST KITTS AND NEVIS

People of Panama
The Kuna are an indigenous people who live on the coasts and islands of Panama and Colombia. They mostly live by fishing and are well known for their craft work, which includes wood carving and the making of molas, the colourful blouses being worn here.

NORTHERN ANDEAN COUNTRIES

THE ANDES MOUNTAINS extend down the whole length of South America, from north to south. They rise in Colombia, the country which borders the narrow land link with Central America, the Isthmus of Panama.

Colombia is a beautiful country with three ranges of the Andes running through it. The mountains slope east to grasslands and then to rainforest. The chief cities are on the coast, which is warm and humid, or in the cooler mountain regions. The mountains are mined for gold, emeralds, salt and coal.

The Andes rise to 6,267 metres above sea level at Chimborazo in **Ecuador**. Bananas and sugar-cane are grown here. In the cooler foothills of the Andes coffee is an important crop. To the east of the mountains are rainforests, where oil is drilled. Ecuador is the second largest oil producer in South America after Venezuela.

In the 1400s, **Peru** was the centre of the mighty Inca empire, an advanced Native American civilization which produced beautiful textiles and jewellery in gold and precious stones. Ruined Inca cities such as Machu Picchu still perch high amongst the peaks of the Andes. Terraced hillsides allow crops such as potatoes to be grown in the mountains. Fishing is important along the foggy Pacific coast. In the far east, rivers flow through tropical forests into the river Amazon.

Lake Titicaca lies high in the Andes on the border between Peru and **Bolivia.** Bolivia is an inland country which lies across the high plateau of the Altiplano, where most Bolivians live, and stretches into hot, humid rainforest in the east. The city of La Paz is the world's highest capital city, at 3,660 metres above sea level. Bolivia produces tin, timber, rubber and potatoes.

The lands of the northern Andes are home to many Native Americans, such as the Quechua and Aymara peoples. The whole region was ruled by Spain from the 1500s to the early 1800s, and Spanish is spoken throughout the region as well as a number of Native

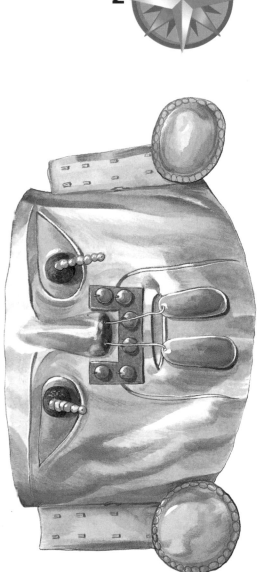

Inca crafts

This mask was made by Inca goldsmiths in Peru. The Incas came to power in the 1400s and were famous for their beautiful work with gold.

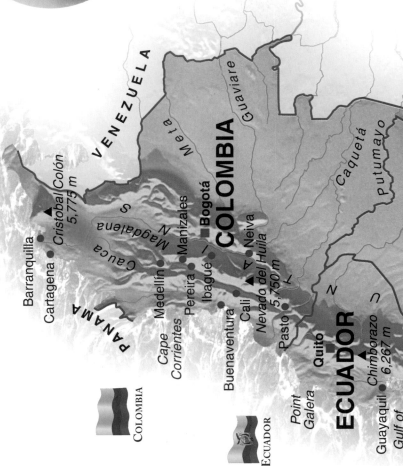

PERU

COLOMBIA

ECUADOR

Point. Gallinas

Barranquilla
Cartagena ● ▲ Cristóbal Colón
5,775 m

VENEZUELA

Meta

Guaviare

Cape
Corrientes
Medellín
Pereira
Manizales
Ibagué ●
Cali ●
Buenaventura
Pasto ●
Point
Galera
Quito
COLOMBIA
Bogotá ■
Neiva ●
▲ Nevado del Huila
5,750 m

Magdalena
Cauca

N

Cauca

S
Caquetá
Putumayo

Amazon

BRAZIL

Iquitos ●

Marañón

ECUADOR
Guayaquil ● ▲ Chimborazo
6,267 m
Gulf of
Guayaquil
Piura ●

PANAMA

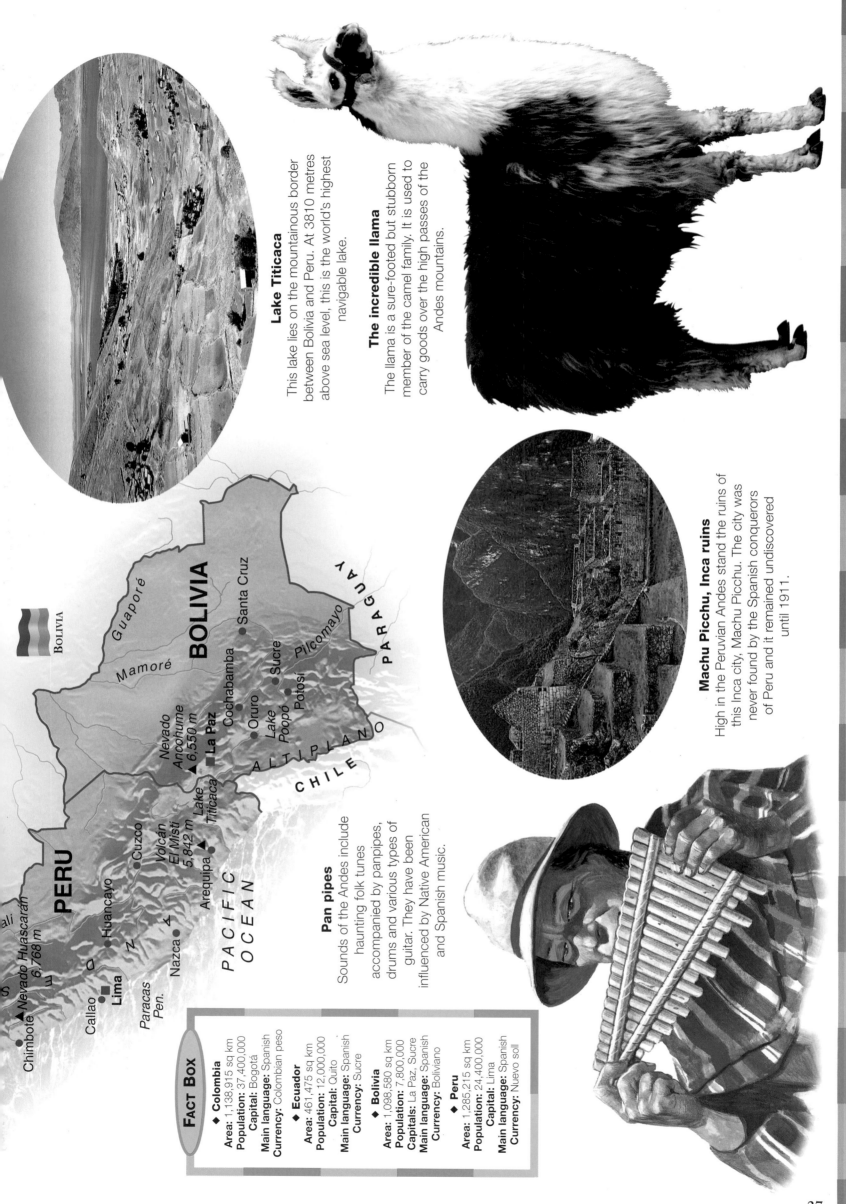

Lake Titicaca

This lake lies on the mountainous border between Bolivia and Peru. At 3810 metres above sea level, this is the world's highest navigable lake.

The incredible llama

The llama is a sure-footed but stubborn member of the camel family. It is used to carry goods over the high passes of the Andes mountains.

Machu Picchu, Inca ruins

High in the Peruvian Andes stand the ruins of this Inca city, Machu Picchu. The city was never found by the Spanish conquerors of Peru and it remained undiscovered until 1911.

Pan pipes

Sounds of the Andes include haunting folk tunes accompanied by panpipes, drums and various types of guitar. They have been influenced by Native American and Spanish music.

FACT BOX

◆ **Colombia**
Area: 1,138,915 sq km
Population: 37,400,000
Capital: Bogotá
Main language: Spanish
Currency: Colombian peso

◆ **Ecuador**
Area: 461,475 sq km
Population: 12,000,000
Capital: Quito
Currency: Sucre

◆ **Bolivia**
Area: 1,098,580 sq km
Population: 7,800,000
Capitals: La Paz, Sucre
Main language: Spanish
Currency: Boliviano

◆ **Peru**
Area: 1,285,215 sq km
Population: 24,400,000
Capital: Lima
Main language: Spanish
Currency: Nuevo soll

BOLIVIA

PERU

BOLIVIA

Guaporé

Mamoré

Santa Cruz

Cochabamba

Pilcomayo

Sucre

Oruro

Potosí

Lake
Poopó

Nevado
Ancohume ▲ 6,550 m ■ La Paz

ALTIPLANO

Lake
Titicaca

CHILE

PARAGUAY

Cuzco

Volcán
El Misti
5,842 m ▲

Arequipa

Huancayo

Nazca

PACIFIC
OCEAN

▲ Nevado Huascarán
6,768 m

Chimbote

Callao

Lima

Paracas
Pen.

ali

Netherlands
Antilles

Gulf of
Venezuela

Maracaibo

Caracas

Barcelona

Lake
Maracaibo ANDES MTS.

LLANOS

Orinoco

Port of Spain **TRINIDAD & TOBAGO**

Orinoco Delta

GUYANA

Pico Bolívar
5,002 m

VENEZUELA

Angel
Falls

Georgetown

GUYANA

Paramaribo

SURINAM

COLOMBIA

G U I A N A   H I G H L A N D S

SURINAM

Cayenne

FRENCH GUIANA

Orinoco

VENEZUELA

Branco

Pico da Neblina
3014 m

Negro

FRENCH
GUIANA

Japurá

Macapá

Marajó
Bay

Marajó I.

Belèm

São
Marcos
Bay

São Luis

Manaus

Amazon

Santarém

S E L V A S

Madeira

Tapajós

Xingu

Tocantins

Teresina

Juruá

Purus

Aripuanã

Araguaia

Parnaiba

Rio Branco

Jiparaná

Arinos

BRAZIL

Sobradinho
Reservoir

PERU

SERRA DOS PARECIS
Guaporé

BOLIVIA

MATO GROSSO
PLATEAU

Cuiabá

Brasília

Goiânia

B R A Z I L I A N
H I G H L A N D S

Uberlandia

Campo Grande

Paraná

Coffee beans
Brazil is the world's biggest producer of
coffee. The crop is mostly grown in the south,
on large estates and is exported worldwide.

Belo Horizonte

Campos

São Paulo

Santos

Rio de
Janeiro

Cape
Frio

Itaipu Res.

Itguaçu
Falls

Curitiba

S E R R A   D O   M A R

BRAZIL

PARAGUAY

ARGENTINA

Uruguay

Florianópolis

N

Santa Maria

Pôrto Alegre

URUGUAY

Patos Lagoon

Mirim Lake

Rio panorama
A huge statue of Christ stands high above the
Brazilian port of Rio de Janeiro.

BRAZIL AND ITS NEIGHBOURS

BRAZIL is South America's largest nation. It includes grasslands, fertile plateaus and dry areas of scrub.

About a third of the country is taken up by tropical rainforests. All kinds of rare plants, parrots, snakes and monkeys live in these dense, dripping forests, which are under threat from road-builders, farmers, miners and loggers. The forests are crossed by hundreds of rivers, which drain into the wide, muddy waters of the Amazon, one of the world's two longest rivers. The river basin of the Amazon is the world's largest, covering 7,045,000 square kilometres.

Most Brazilians live in the big cities of the Atlantic coast, such as Rio de Janeiro and São Paolo. The country has rich resources, but many of the population are poor people who live in shacks built on the outskirts of the city. Brasília, with its broad avenues and high-rise buildings, was specially built as the country's new capital city in the 1960s.

To the northeast of Brazil, on the Caribbean coast, is **Venezuela**. This land, crossed by the Orinoco River, includes rainforests, high mountains and the tropical grassy plains of the Llanos. The beautiful Angel Falls (the world's highest at 979 metres) provide hydroelectric power, while Lake Maracaibo, in the northwest, is rich in oil.

The three other countries on the Caribbean coast are **Guyana**, **Surinam** and **French Guiana**. The first was once a British colony, the second was a Dutch colony and the third is still an overseas department governed by France. Most people live in the humid regions of the coast, while the rainforests and mountains of the remote south are more sparsely populated. Crops include sugar-cane, coffee, rice and bananas. An important mineral is bauxite, used in the making of aluminium.

Many different ethnic groups live in the region as a whole, including Native American peoples who have had to struggle to survive ever since Europeans invaded the region in the 1500s. The population of northern South America also includes many people of Asian, African, European and mixed descent, with ancestors from Spain, Portugal, Italy, Germany, France, Netherlands and Britain.

FACT BOX

◆ **Brazil**
Area: 8,511,965 sq km
Population: 160,300,000
Capital: Brasília
Main language: Portuguese
Currency: Cruzeiro real

◆ **Venezuela**
Area: 912,045 sq km
Population: 22,600,000
Capital: Caracas
Main language: Spanish
Currency: Bolívar

◆ **Guyana**
Area: 214,970 sq km
Population: 800,000
Capital: Georgetown
Main language: English
Currency: Guyana dollar

◆ **Surinam**
Area: 163,820 sq km
Population: 446,000
Capital: Paramaribo
Official language: Dutch
Currency: Surinam guilder

◆ **French Guiana**
Area: 91,000 sq km
Population: 300,000
Capital: Cayenne
Main language: French
Currency: French franc

(Map labels: rtaleza, Natal, SERTÃO, Recife, São Francisco, Maceió, lvador)

Rainforest creatures
The vast forests which are drained by the River Amazon, support all kinds of wildlife, such as this brightly coloured macaw. Sadly, many species are threatened by the clearance of the forests by farmers and illegal traders in wildlife.

Fishing for a living
A fishing crew check their tackle as children play on the beach. This scene is near Salvador, capital of the tropical Bahía region in northeastern Brazil.

Yanomami hunters
About 13,000 Yanomami people live in Venezuela and another 8000 in Brazil. They live by hunting, fishing and growing food in the rainforest.

ARGENTINA AND ITS NEIGHBOURS

THE SOUTHERN PART of South America stretches from the hot and humid Gran Chaco region to the cold and stormy waters of Tierra del Fuego and Cape Horn.

The largest country of this region is **Argentina**. Its highly populated capital is Buenos Aires on the river Plate. More than eight out of every ten Argentineans are city dwellers. However it was the country's cattle-farming regions – the Pampa grasslands and the northeast – that in the last 150 years brought wealth to the country and attracted large numbers of settlers from Europe. Argentina's western borders follow the high peak of the Andes range, which reach their highest point at Cerro Aconcagua (6,959 metres above sea level). To the south are the windswept plateaus of Patagonia, largely given over to sheep farming. The port of Ushuaia is the southernmost town in the world.

Northwards from Buenos Aires, across the river Plate, lies Montevideo, capital of **Uruguay**. This is another country which raises cattle and sheep, and whose rich grasslands and mild climate attracted European settlers. Neighbouring **Paraguay** is far from the coast. Most of its people farm the hills and plains of the east. Few live in the hot wilderness of the Gran Chaco.

To the west of the Andes is **Chile**, which covers a long and narrow area. Here is one of the driest regions on Earth, the Atacama desert. It also includes fertile orchards and productive vineyards, the big city of Santiago and the spectacular glaciers of the southern Andes. Spanish is spoken throughout the region, and some Native American languages such as Guaraní may also be heard.

Armadillo

The head and body of the armadillo is covered by an armour of plates made of horny and bony material. These usually nocturnal animals, feed mainly on insects and rest in a burrow by day.

Paraná River, Paraguay

Separating Paraguay and Argentina the Parana River flows some 4,500 km. The English explorer Sebastian Cabot was the first to sail up it in 1526.

BRAZIL

PARAGUAY

URUGUAY

BOLIVIA

CHILE

PARAGUAY

Concepción

Cuidad del Este

Asunción

Verde

Pilcomayo

Bermejo

G R A N C H A C O

Formosa

Alto Paraná

Paraguay

Posadas

Corrientes

Resistencia

Salto

Paysandú

Concordia

Negro

MESOPOTAMIA

Paraná

Uruguay

Salta

San Miguel de Tucumán

Santiago del Estero

Catamarca

La Rioja

Salado

Mar Chiquito

Córdoba

Santa Fe

Paraná

Rosario

SIERRA DE CÓRDOBA

Río Cuarto

San Luis

Calama

Copiapó

Ojos del Salado
6,880 m

San Juan

Mendoza

Aconcagua
6,959 m

Santiago

Arica

Iquique

Antofagasta

ATACAMA DESERT

Coquimbo

Pta. Lengua de Vaca

Valparaíso

FACT BOX

◆ **Argentina**
Area: 2,780,090 sq km
Population: 35,600,000
Capital: Buenos Aires
Official language: Spanish
Currency: Peso

◆ **Chile**
Area: 736,000 sq km
Population: 14,600,000
Capital: Santiago
Official language: Spanish
Currency: Peso

◆ **Paraguay**
Area: 406,750 sq km
Population: 5,100,000
Capital: Asunción
Official language: Spanish
Currency: Guarani

◆ **Uruguay**
Area: 176,210 sq km
Population: 3,200,000
Capital: Montevideo
Official language: Spanish
Currency: Peso

Prickly Pear

The flesh and seeds of the peeled fruit of the prickly pear have a pleasant taste. This cactus is low-growing and has flat oval stem joints and bright yellow flowers and occurs in Central and South America.

SOUTH GEORGIA (U.K.)

N

Buenos Aires by night

The Monument of the Two Congresses stands in front of the domed Palace of Congress, built in 1906. The Argentinian capital is a large, lively city.

URUGUAY

ARGENTINA

Cape San Antonio
Mar del Plata
Cape Corrientes

ARGENTINA

Bahía Blanca
Bahía Blanca
Viedma
San Matías Gulf
Valdés Peninsula
Rawson

Colorado
Negro
Neuquén
Limay

Chillán
Concepción
Pta. Lavapié

CHILE

Temuco

Valdivia
Pta. de la Galera
Osorno
Puerto Montt

Chiloé I.
C. Quilán

LOS CHONOS
ARCHIPELAGO

Penas
Gulf

PACIFIC
OCEAN

Wellington I.

REINA ADELAIDA
ARCHIPELAGO

Santa Inés I.

P A T A G O N I A
A N D E S

Chico
Chubut
Chico
Deseado
Lake Buenos
Aires

Comodoro Rivadavia
San Jorge Gulf
C. Tres Puntas
Puerto Deseado

Santa Cruz
Puerto Santa Cruz

Bahía
Grande
Río Gallegos
Strait of Magellan
Punta Arenas
Tierra
del
Fuego
Ushuaia
C. San Diego

Cape Horn

FALKLAND/MALVINAS
ISLANDS

West
Falkland

Stanley
East
Falkland

Mountains, Southern Chile

The long, narrow country of Chile has vast differences in climate. There is hot desert in the north, Mediterranean type in the centre and cool, humid conditions in the south. Some mountains are permanently snow-capped.

Turkish women
These women are from the port of Kas in southern Turkey. They are kneading dough and making pastry. Many Muslim women cover their heads with scarves or full veils.

ASIA

SOUTHWEST ASIA

SOUTHWEST ASIA IS SOMETIMES described as the Near East or the Middle East. Its peoples include Greek Cypriots, Turks, Jews, Arabs, Kurds and Iranians.

The region has seen many political disputes and wars in recent years – between Greeks and Turks on Cyprus, between Palestinian Arabs and Jews in Israel, between Iraqi and Iranians and between Iraqui and Kuwaiti Arabs. The Kurds, whose homeland is occupied by **Iraq**, **Iran** and **Turkey**, have also been at the centre of conflict.

It was in Southwest Asia that the world's first civilizations grew up, between the rivers Tigris and Euphrates, over 6,000 years ago. The region later gave birth to three world faiths – Judaism, Christianity and Islam. In the days of the Roman empire the Jews were scattered from their homeland, and over the centuries their culture spread to Spain, Central and Eastern Europe and the Americas. Arab armies and traders took the Islamic faith into Africa and Spain, and Arab scholars made great advances in mathematics and astronomy. From the 1500s the Turks established a great empire which stretched from Central Europe to the Indian Ocean.

Southwest Asia includes vast deserts, in the Arabian peninsula and in eastern Iran. It also takes in fertile plains, the marshes of southern Iraq and mountain ranges of Turkey and Iran. The north of the region borders the Black Sea and the Caspian Sea, grassy steppes and the Caucasus mountains. To the east lies Afghanistan, Pakistan and the Indian sub-continent.

The region's most valuable resource is oil, which brings wealth to the governments of the lands around the Persian Gulf. However many ordinary people of Southwest Asia remain poor, living by herding goats, sheep or camels. In Israel and some other regions irrigation has made it possible to grow crops in harsh, dry environments. Oranges, dates, grapes and many kinds of nuts are grown in the region.

A summons to prayer
Mosques, like this one in Kuwait, have tall towers called minarets. From here, faithful Muslims are called to prayer. This message is often broadcast from loudspeakers. Muslims are expected to pray five times a day.

Map labels:
Istanbul, TURKEY, SYRIA, Samsun, BLACK SEA, PONTIC MOUNTAINS, Gallipoli, Sakarya, Bursa, Eskisehir, Ankara, Kizil, Izmir, Tuz Lake, TURKEY, Lake Van, Kayseri, Konya, Gaziantep, Diyarbakir, TAURUS MTS., Adana, Antalya, Aleppo, Mosul, CYPRUS, Nicosia, CYPRUS, SYRIA, Euphrates, Limassol, Tripoli, Homs, LEBANON, SYRIAN DESERT, LEBANON, Beirut, Damascus, Haifa, IRAQ, ISRAEL, Tel Aviv, Amman, Kar, Jerusalem, JORDAN, ISRAEL, EGYPT, Elat, Al Jawf, Sakakah, AN NAFU, JORDAN, Buray, HIJAZ, Medina, RED, SAUD, Jiddah, Mecca, SEA, ASIR, Tihamah, Jabal Sa, 3,133, Jaza'ir Farasan, SAUDI ARABIA, Al Hudayd, Bab al M

Wealth from oil
These supertankers are taking oil on board, off the coast of Saudi Arabia. Wealth from oil has transformed the economy of the Middle East and given great power to the many small countries around the Persian Gulf.

IRAQ

N

KUWAIT

BAHRAIN

IRAN

QATAR

UNITED ARAB EMIRATES

OMAN

YEMEN

Ararat
185 m

Aras

Tabriz

CASPIAN SEA

Rasht

Babol

ELBURZ MTS.

▲ Mt. Damavand
5,604 m

Lake Urmia

As Sulaymaniyah

Mashhad

Hamadan

Tehran

kuk

Bakhtaran

Qom

Kashan

Dasht-e-Kavir

IRAN

ZAGROS MOUNTAINS

ghdad

Esfahan

Dasht-e-Lut

AFGHANISTAN

Yazd

An Nasiriyah

Ahvaz

TURKMENISTAN

Kerman

Basra

Abadan

Shiraz

Zahedan

KUWAIT

Kuwait

Bushehr

Ad Dahna

Bandar Abbas

Ad Damman

Bandar e Lengeh

Strait of Hormuz

Jask

Al Manamah

Gulf of Oman

BAHRAIN

QATAR

Dubai

aqra

Doha

Abu Dhabi

Muscat

Riyadh

UNITED ARAB EMIRATES

Jabal Ash Sham
3,035 m

Sur

RABIA

OMAN

(Rub' al Khali (Empty Quarter))

Masirah I.

On the move
In many parts of Southwest Asia people live as nomads, wandering with their herds from one pasture to another, or following ancient trade routes.

Salalah

Kuria Muria Is.

Tarim

Hadramaut

n'a

YEMEN

Al Mukalla

Gulf of Aden

Socotra (YEMEN)

'Abd al kuri

FACT BOX

◆ **Cyprus**
Area: 9,250 sq km
Population: 725,000
Capital: Nicosia
Official languages: Greek, Turkish
Currency: Cyprus pound

◆ **Lebanon**
Area: 10,400 sq km
Population: 3,900,000
Capital: Beirut
Official language: Arabic
Currency: Lebanese pound

◆ **Israel**
Area: 20,770 sq km
Population: 5,800,000
Capital: Jerusalem
Official languages: Hebrew, Arabic
Currency: Shekel

◆ **Jordan**
Area: 96,000 sq km
Population: 4,400,000
Capital: Amman
Official language: Arabic
Currency: Jordanian dinar

◆ **Syria**
Area: 185,680 sq km
Population: 15,000,000
Capital: Damascus
Official language: Arabic
Currency: Syrian pound

◆ **Turkey**
Area: 779,450 sq km
Population: 63,700,000
Capital: Ankara
Official language: Turkish
Currency: Turkish lira

◆ **Iraq**
Area: 438,445 sq km
Population: 21,2000,000
Capital: Baghdad
Official language: Arabic
Currency: Iraqi dinar

◆ **Iran**
Area: 1,648,000 sq km
Population: 67,500,000
Capital: Tehran
Official language: Farsi
Currency: Rial

◆ **United Arab Emirates**
Area: 75,150 sq km
Population: 2,300,000
Capital: Abu Dhabi
Official language: Arabic
Currency: Dirham

◆ **Qatar**
Area: 11,435 sq km
Population: 600,000
Capital: Doha
Official language: Arabic
Currency: Qatari rial

◆ **Oman**
Area: 271,950 sq km
Population: 2,300,000
Capital: Muscat
Official language: Arabic
Currency: Omani rial

◆ **Yemen**
Area: 527,970 sq km
Population: 15,200,000
Capital: San'a
Official language: Arabic
Currencies: Yemeni riyal, dinar

◆ **Saudi Arabia**
Area: 2,400,900 sq km
Population: 19,500,000
Capital: Riyadh
Official language: Arabic
Currency: Saudi riyal

◆ **Kuwait**
Area: 24,280 sq km
Population: 1,800,000
Capital: Kuwait City
Official language: Arabic
Currency: Kuwaiti dinar

◆ **Bahrain**
Area: 661 sq km
Population: 600,000
Capital: Manamah
Official language: Arabic
Currency: Bahraini dinar

INDIA AND ITS NEIGHBOURS

SOUTHERN ASIA stretches south into the Indian Ocean, forming a landmass so large that it sometimes called the 'sub-continent'. Its northern limits are marked by the Himalaya and Karakoram mountain ranges. These include many of the world's highest peaks and reach 8,848 metres above sea level at Everest, on Nepal's border with China.

The ranges pass through eastern Afghanistan, the Kashmir region on the border of India and Pakistan, India itself and the small mountain kingdoms of **Nepal** and **Bhutan**. Melting snows flow south from the mountains to form the five great rivers of the Punjab and also the mighty Ganges, which winds across the fertile plains of northern India before crossing Bangladesh into a maze of waterways around the Bay of Bengal. This area suffers from devastating floods.

Central and southern **India** form a triangular plateau called the Deccan, fringed on the east and west by the mountainous Ghats. These slopes are forested, catching the full force of the monsoon winds which bring rains from the Indian Ocean. For most of the year India is extremely hot and dry. Indian Ocean nations include the beautiful, tropical island of **Sri Lanka** and a chain of very low coral islands, the **Maldives**.

Advanced civilizations had developed around the river Indus by about 2500BC, and great religions grew up in India over the ages, including Hinduism, Buddhism and Sikhism. Invaders and traders brought Islam to the region. India today is a fascinating mixture of cultures, with over 800 different languages and dialects. There are many different customs, dress and foods. Spicy dishes from India are now popular everywhere.

The Indian sub-continent has a vast population, with many hungry mouths to feed. Many people make their living by farming, growing wheat, rice, millet, sugar-cane, coconut and tea. Most industries are based in the highly populated cities of India and Pakistan.

Himalayan peaks

Breathtaking Mount Makalu, on the border between Nepal and China, rises to 8,470 metres above sea level. Eighty-eight percent of the world's mountains over 7,315 metres rise within the Himalaya-Karakoram ranges, many of them in the kingdom of Nepal.

AFGHANISTAN

PAKISTAN

TURKMENISTAN

TAJIKISTAN

AFGHANISTAN

HINDU

Mazar-e-Sharif

Kabul

Khyber Pass

Peshawar

Farah

Qandahar

Quetta

Herat

RIGESTAN DESERT

BALUCHISTAN PLATEAU

PAKISTAN

SULAIMAN RANGE

Islamabad

Rawalpindi

Faisalabad

Lahore

Multan

Bahawalpur

Sukkur

Indus

Hyderabad

Karachi

Gulf of K

Sutlej

GREAT INDIAN DESERT (THAR DESERT)

DISPUTED AREA

K2 8,611m

KARAKORAM

Srinagar

JAMMU & KASHMIR

Amritsar

PUNJAB

Jodhpur

Udaipur

Ajmer

Kota

Jaipur

Gwalior

Delhi

New Delhi

Agra

Yamuna

Nanda Devi 7,817m

Tibet (CHINA)

NEPAL

Annapurna 8,078m

Mt Everest 8,848m

Katmandu

Ghaghara

Lucknow

Kanpur

Bareilly

NEPAL

Thimphu

BHUTAN

BHUTAN

Brahmaputra

GA HILLS

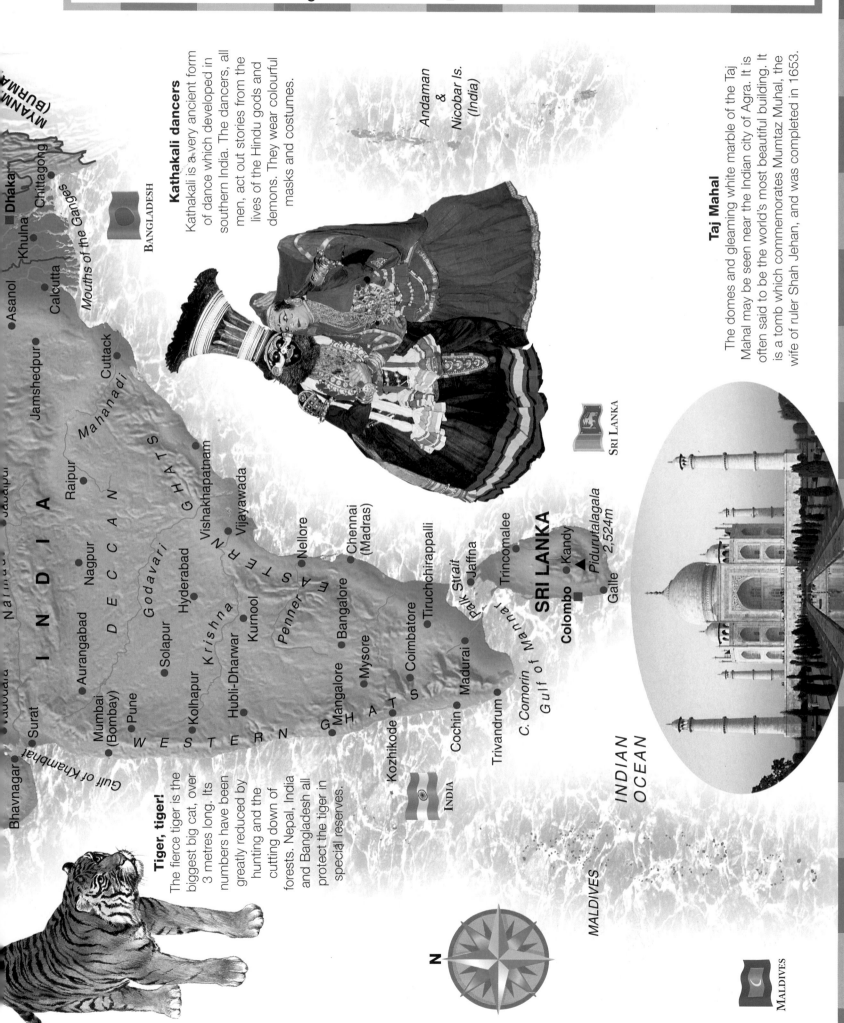

FACT BOX

◆ **Afghanistan**
Area: 652,225 sq km
Population: 22,100,000
Capital: Kabul
Official languages: Pushtu, Dari
Currency: Afghani

◆ **Bangladesh**
Area: 144,000 sq km
Population: 122,210,000
Capital: Dhaka
Official language: Bengali
Currency: Taka

◆ **Bhutan**
Area: 46,620 sq km
Population: 800,000
Capital: Thimphu
Official languages: Dzongkha, English
Currency: Ngultrum

◆ **India**
Area: 3,166,830 sq km
Population: 969,700,000
Capital: Delhi
Official languages: Hindi, Assamese, Bengali, Gujarati, Kannarese, Kashmiri, Malayalam, Marathi, Oriya, Punjabi, Sanskrit, Sindhi, Tamil, Telugu, Urdu, Nepali
Currency: Indian rupee

◆ **Maldives**
Area: 298 sq km
Population: 300,000
Capital: Malé
Official language: Divehi
Currency: Rufiyaa

◆ **Nepal**
Area: 141,415m sq km
Population: 22,600,000
Capital: Kathmandu
Official language: Nepali
Currency: Nepalese rupee

◆ **Pakistan**
Area: 803,940 sq km
Population: 137,800,000
Capital: Islamabad
Official language: Urdu
Currency: Pakistani rupee

◆ **Sri Lanka**
Area: 65,610 sq km
Population: 18,700,000
Capital: Colombo
Official language: Sinhalese, Tamil
Currency: Sri Lankan rupee

Kathakali dancers

Kathakali is a very ancient form of dance which developed in southern India. The dancers, all men, act out stories from the lives of the Hindu gods and demons. They wear colourful masks and costumes.

Taj Mahal

The domes and gleaming white marble of the Taj Mahal may be seen near the Indian city of Agra. It is often said to be the world's most beautiful building. It is a tomb which commemorates Mumtaz Muhal, the wife of ruler Shah Jehan, and was completed in 1653.

Tiger, tiger!

The fierce tiger is the biggest big cat, over 3 metres long. Its numbers have been greatly reduced by hunting and the cutting down of forests. Nepal, India and Bangladesh all protect the tiger in special reserves.

MYANMAR (BURMA)

Dhaka
Chittagong
Khulna
Asanol
Calcutta
Jamshedpur
Cuttack
Mouths of the Ganges

BANGLADESH

Raipur
Nagpur
Aurangabad
Hyderabad
Solapur
Kolhapur
Kurnool
Hubli-Dharwar
Mumbai (Bombay)
Pune
Surat
Bhavnagar
Gulf of Khambhat

I N D I A

D E C C A N

Narmada
Godavari
Krishna
Penner
Mahanadi

G H A T S

E A S T E R N

W E S T E R N   G H A T S

Vishakhapatnam
Vijayawada
Nellore
Chennai (Madras)
Bangalore
Mysore
Mangalore
Coimbatore
Tiruchchirappalli
Madurai
Cochin
Kozhikode
Trivandrum

Palk Strait
Jaffna
Trincomalee
Kandy
Pidurutalagala 2,524m
Galle
Colombo

SRI LANKA

C. Comorin
Gulf of Mannar

INDIA

SRI LANKA

Andaman & Nicobar Is. (India)

MALDIVES

INDIAN OCEAN

MALDIVES

N

45

ASIA

CHINA AND ITS NEIGHBOURS

CHINA is the world's third largest country in area, and has a higher population than any other. It is bordered by the world's highest mountains, by deserts and by tropical seas.

Most people live in the big industrial cities of the south and east and on the fertile plains around two great rivers, the Huang He and the Chiang Jiang. Crops include wheat, maize, tea, sugar-cane and rice. Rice is eaten with almost every meal. Chinese civilization dates back over thousands of years. Chinese inventions included paper and gunpowder and Chinese crafts included the making of fine porcelain and silk. Since 1949 China has been ruled by its Communist Party, but its politics are no longer really socialist. Its economy has become one of the most important in the Pacific region, and in 1997 it took back the territory of Hong Kong, an international centre of business which had been a British colony. China also claims the island of **Taiwan**, which is still governed independently by Chinese nationalists who lost power in 1949.

The **Korean peninsula** saw bitter fighting between 1950 and 1953, when Korea divided into two nations, North and South. These countries remain bitter enemies today. South Korea has become an important industrial power.

Far to the north the Mongol peoples live in the independent republic of **Mongolia**. This includes the barren Gobi desert and remote grasslands.

Ulaangom
Hovd
Fuhai
KAZAKHSTAN
ALTAI MTS.
Ebinur Hu
Karamay
Dzungaria
Yining
Kuytun
Ürümqi
Hami
KYRGYZSTAN
TIAN SHAN
Aksu
Bosten Lake
Turfan Depress
Kashi
Yur
TAKLIMAKAN DESERT
ALTUN SHAN
Hotan
KUNLUN SHAN
Mt. K2
KARAKORAM
PLATEAU OF TIBET
Siling Lake
TANGGULA SI
INDIA
HIM
Tangra Lake
Nam Lake
Lhasa
Mt. Everest 8,848 m
Xigaze
NEPAL
L
A
Y
A
BHUTAN

The Great Wall
A defensive wall runs across the north of China for about 6,000 kilometres, with many extra twists and turns. It was started in about 246 BC and added to over hundreds of years.

Temple of Heaven
Tiantan, the Temple of Heaven in Beijing, is a beautiful group of buildings first raised in 1420. The Chinese emperors used to come here to pray for a good harvest.

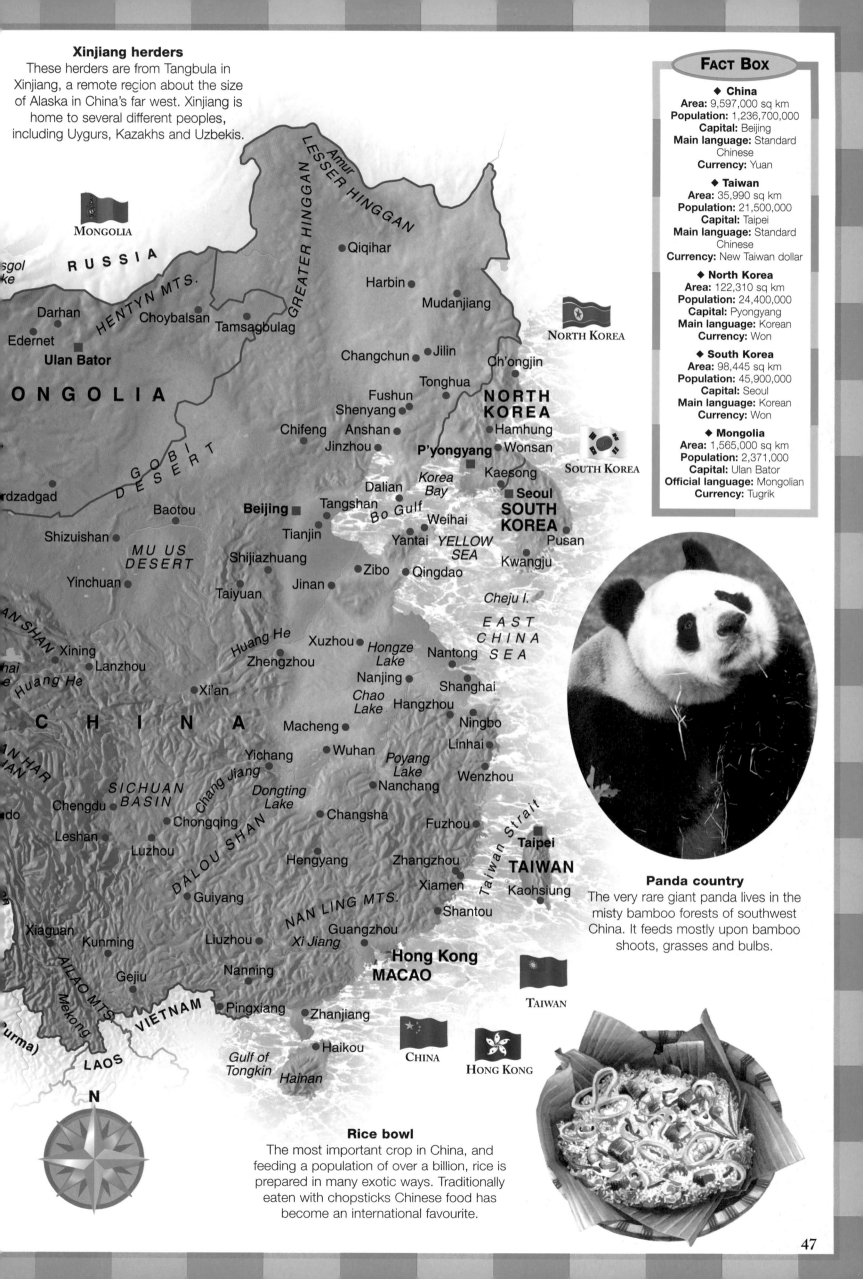

Xinjiang herders
These herders are from Tangbula in Xinjiang, a remote region about the size of Alaska in China's far west. Xinjiang is home to several different peoples, including Uygurs, Kazakhs and Uzbekis.

MONGOLIA

RUSSIA

Amur
LESSER HINGGAN
GREATER HINGGAN

HENTYN MTS.

sgol
ke
Darhan
Edernet
Choybalsan
Tamsagbulag
Ulan Bator

Qiqihar
Harbin
Mudanjiang

Changchun • Jilin
Ch'ongjin

Tonghua

NORTH
KOREA

M O N G O L I A

GOBI
DESERT

rdzadgad

Baotou
Shizuishan

MU US
DESERT

Yinchuan

Fushun
Shenyang
Chifeng Anshan
Jinzhou

Dalian
Tangshan
Bo Gulf

Hamhung
Wonsan

P'yongyang
Kaesong

Korea
Bay

Weihai
Yantai YELLOW
SEA
Zibo Qingdao

Seoul
SOUTH
KOREA

NORTH KOREA

SOUTH KOREA

Beijing
Tianjin
Shijiazhuang
Taiyuan
Jinan

Pusan

Kwangju

Cheju I.

EAST
CHINA
SEA

AN SHAN
hai
Xining
Lanzhou
Huang He

C H I N A

Huang He

Xi'an

Xuzhou
Zhengzhou
Hongze
Lake
Nanjing
Chao
Lake
Nantong
Hangzhou

Shanghai

Ningbo
Linhai

Macheng

Yichang • Wuhan
Poyang
Lake
Nanchang

Wenzhou

AN HAR
AN
do

SICHUAN
BASIN

Chang Jiang

Dongting
Lake

Chengdu
Chongqing
Leshan
Luzhou

DALOU SHAN

Changsha

Fuzhou

Taiwan Strait

Taipei
TAIWAN

Hengyang
Zhangzhou
Xiamen
Kaohsiung
Shantou

Guiyang

NAN LING MTS.

Xiaguan
Kunming
Gejiu
AILAO MTS

Liuzhou
Guangzhou
Xi Jiang

Hong Kong
MACAO

Nanning

Mekong

VIETNAM

Pingxiang
Zhanjiang

TAIWAN

CHINA
HONG KONG

urma)
LAOS

N

Haikou
Gulf of
Tongkin
Hainan

Panda country
The very rare giant panda lives in the misty bamboo forests of southwest China. It feeds mostly upon bamboo shoots, grasses and bulbs.

Rice bowl
The most important crop in China, and feeding a population of over a billion, rice is prepared in many exotic ways. Traditionally eaten with chopsticks Chinese food has become an international favourite.

JAPAN

JAPAN is made up of over 3,000 islands, and these stretch for about 3,000 kilometres from north to south on the northwest rim of the Pacific Ocean.

The chief islands are called Hokkaido, Honshu, Shikoku and Kyushu. The islands extend from the tropical south to the chilly north, where winter snowfalls can be heavy. The region is a danger zone for earthquakes and Japan's highest mountain, Fuji, is a volcano.

The snow-covered slopes of Mount Fuji have been a favourite subject for Japanese artists over the years. Japan has a long history of excellence in art, theatre, poetry, architecture and pottery. Japanese civilization dates back over 2,000 years. The country has been ruled by emperors and, during the Middle Ages, it was fought over by powerful warlords and bands of knights called samurai. Faiths include Buddhism and Shinto, the country's traditional religion.

Japan is very mountainous and so land that is suitable for farming is very precious. Japanese farmers grow rice, tea and fruit and the country also has a large fishing fleet. Many meals are based on rice or fish. Japan has very few natural resources. Even so, over the last 50 years Japan has become a leading world producer of cars, televisions and other electrical goods.

The mountains also limit the spread of housing and so Japan's cities are mostly crowded on to the strip of flat land around the coast. Tokyo has spread out to join up with neighbouring cities, and now has a population of over 25 million.

The Japanese people make up 99 percent of the country's population. The remainder includes Koreans and the Ainu of the far north, who may be descended from the first people to inhabit Japan.

Mount Fuji

The beautiful peak of Mount Fuji, to the southwest of Tokyo, is a national symbol and, traditionally, a sacred mountain.

Sushi

Prawns, raw fish, seaweed, pickles and vegetables are used to make these tasty snacks. Like most Japanese dishes, they are served with rice. Japanese food is often beautifully arranged and thoughtfully served.

Tea time

Tea is harvested on the inland slopes. The Japanese are great tea-drinkers and have an ancient ceremony

JAPAN

Kuril Is. (Russia)

La Pérouse Strait

Wakkanai

Rebun I.

Rishiri I.

H o k k a i d o

Teshio

Asahigawa

▲ Asahi Mt. 2,290 m

Kushiro

Obihiro

Ishikari

Erimo Cape

Otaru

Ishikari Bay

Sapporo

Muroran

Uchiura Bay

Hakodate

Tsugaru Strait

Mutsa Bay

Aomori

Hachinohe

Hirosaki

S E A O F J A P A N

Akita

Morioka

Kitak

Itsukushima, Japan

Japan has many ancient Shinto shrines and Buddhist temples and many of these are set in beautiful scenery or gardens. Japan has always produced very simple and beautiful architecture and design.

Sumo wrestlers

The ancient sport of sumo is still very popular in Japan. Super heavyweight wrestlers aim to ground their opponents or force them out of the ring. There are long ceremonies before each contest.

Ride the Bullet

Japan's Bullet Train offers one of the world's most famous passenger express services. It speeds across the country, linking the capital, Tokyo, with other large cities.

A Shinto wedding

Dressed in her beautiful silk robe, or kimono, a Japanese bride sits next to her new husband, who also wears traditional costume. The wedding has been a Shinto ceremony. Shinto is an ancient Japanese faith which honours ancestors and the spirits of nature.

Map labels

Sendai
Iwaki
Hitachi
Abukuma
Mito
Yamagata
Fukushima
Koriyama
Chiba
Tokyo
Niigata
Utsunomiya
Yokohama
Sado
Nagaoka
Takasaki
Kawasaki
Sagami Bay
Kofu
Mt. Fuji 3,776 m
O-shima
Toyama
Ueda
Matsumoto
Shizuoka
Miyake I.
Kanazawa
Toyota
Hamamatsu
Hachijo I.
Fukui
Gifu
Nagoya
JAPANESE ALPS Shinano
Takefu
Biwa Lake
Kyoto
Osaka
Matsusaka
Oki Is.
Kobe
Sakai
Wakayama
Matsue
Okayama
Kii Channel
Honshu
Inland Sea
Takamatsu
Tokushima
Shikoku
Hiroshima
Suo Sea
Matsuyama
Kochi
Tsushima
Bungo Channel
Kitakyushu
Fukuoka
Sasebo
Omuta
Kumamoto
Kyushu
Amakusa Is.
Sendai
Miyazaki
Nagasaki
Koshiki Is.
Kagoshima
Tanega
Yaku

JAPAN

PACIFIC OCEAN

N

SOUTHEAST ASIA

MYANMAR is a beautiful land lying between the hill country of India and China. It is crossed by the great Irrawaddy river, which flows south into the Indian Ocean. To the southeast is **Thailand**, a country green with rice fields and teak forests. To the west lie the lands once known as Indo-China – **Laos**, **Cambodia** and, on the long Mekong River, **Vietnam**.

Linked to the Asian mainland by a narrow isthmus, or strip of land, is **Malaysia**. This country also takes up the northern part of the island of **Borneo**, which it shares with the small oil-rich state of **Brunei**. Malaysia produces rubber, rice, tea and palm oil. Kuala Lumpur is a growing centre of international business with the 452 metre-high Petronas Towers, the world's highest building. **Singapore**, a small independent city state built on the islands across the Johor Strait, is another leader in the business world.

Indonesia makes up the world's largest island chain. It covers over 13,600 islands, which include Sumatra, Java, southern Borneo, Bali and Irian Jaya (the western half of New Guinea). Another large island chain, the **Philippines**, lie between the Pacific and the South China Sea.

All the islands bordering the Pacific Ocean lie in a danger zone for earthquakes and volcanoes. The region as a whole has a warm, often humid, climate, with monsoon winds bringing heavy rains. Southeast Asia's dwindling tropical forests are a last reserve for the region's rich wildlife, such as enormous butterflies and giant apes called orang-utans.

Many different peoples live in Southeast Asia, including Burmese, Thais, Vietnamese and Filippinos. There are also many people of Chinese and Indian descent. Buddhism is a major faith in the region. Most Indonesians are Muslims and the Philippines are largely Roman Catholic. During the last 50 years Southeast Asia has been torn apart by wars. The region now looks forward to a period of peace.

The face of a demon
This fierce-looking demon guards the gate of the Grand Palace in Bangkok, the capital of Thailand. Many tourists come to this kingdom, once known as Siam, to see its ancient temples and enjoy its beautiful scenery and beaches.

A dome of gold
The fantastic roofs of Shwe Dagon pagoda shimmer with gold. This holy site is in Yangon, capital city of Myanmar or Burma. The pagoda honours Gautama Buddha, the founder of the Buddhist faith.

FACT BOX

◆ **Myanmar (Burma)**
Area: 678,030 sq km
Population: 46,800,000
Capital: Yangon (Rangoon)
Official language: Myanmar (Burmese)
Currency: Kyat

◆ **Thailand**
Area: 514,000 sq km
Population: 60,100,000
Capital: Bangkok
Official language: Thai
Currency: Baht

◆ **Laos**
Area: 236,725 sq km
Population: 5,100,000
Capital: Vientiane
Official language: Lao
Currency: Kip

◆ **Cambodia**
Area: 181,000 sq km
Population: 11,200,000
Capital: Phnom Penh
Official language: Khmer
Currency: Riel

◆ **Vietnam**
Area: 329,565 sq km
Population: 75,100,000
Capital: Hanoi
Official language: Vietnamese
Currency: Dong

◆ **Malaysia**
Area: 332,965 sq km
Population: 21,000,000
Capital: Kuala Lumpur
Official language: Bahasa Malaysia
Currency: Ringgit (Malay dollar)

◆ **Singapore**
Area: 616 sq km
Population: 3,500,000
Capital: Singapore City
Official languages: English, Chinese, Malay, Tamil
Currency: Singapore dollar

◆ **Indonesia**
Area: 1,919,445 sq km
Population: 204,300,000
Capital: Djakarta
Official language: Bahasa Indonesia
Currency: Rupiah

◆ **Brunei**
Area: 5,765 sq km
Population: 276,000
Capital: Bandar Seri Begawan
Official language: Malay
Currency: Ringgit (Brunei dollar)

◆ **Philippines**
Area: 300,000 sq km
Population: 73,400,000
Capital: Manila
Official language: Filipino
Currency: Peso

Javanese carving

These beautiful figures, carved from stone, decorate Barobodur, on the island of Java. This 9th-century temple is the most splendid in Indonesia. Its carvings show scenes from the life of the Buddha.

Floating market

At a Thai market, fruit, vegetables or fish may be sold from small boats. These women traders wear broad-brimmed straw hats to protect them from the tropical sun and the heavy monsoon rains.

Kuala Lumpur

High-rise buildings are influenced by traditional styles in Kuala Lumpur, capital of Malaysia. 'KL' is one of the most important centres of industry, and business in Southeast Asia.

Komodo dragon

Meet the biggest lizard in the world, 3 metres long and weighing in at up to 136 kilograms. It is found on four small islands in Indonesia, called Rintja, Flores, Padar and Komodo.

Map labels:
PHILIPPINES — Laoag, Luzon, Mt. Pinatubo, Manila, Mindoro, Panay, Iloilo, Tacloban, Palawan, Negros, Cebu City, Bohol, SULU SEA, Mindanao, Davao, Zamboanga, Mt. Apo 2,954 m

BRUNEI

INDONESIA — Mt. Kinabalu 4,094 m, Sandakan, SABAH, Bandar Seri gawan, BRUNEI, SARAWAK, BORNEO, Balikpapan, Barito, Banjarmasin, Makassar Strait, Palu, Sulawesi, Ujung Pandang, Baubau, FLORES SEA, Surabaya, Bali, Lombok, Sumbawa, Sumba, Ende, Flores, Timor, Kupang, CELEBES SEA, Manado, MOLUCCA SEA, Halmahera, Moluccas, Sorong, CERAM SEA, Seram, Buru, Ambon, BANDA SEA, Wetar, Tanimbar Islands, Aru Is.

IRIAN JAYA — Puncak Jaya 5,030m, NEW GUINEA, Jayapura, Digul, PAPUA NEW GUINEA

N

Water for sale
A Berber water seller walks the streets of Marrakech, in Morocco, offering metal cups to passers-by.

NORTH AND WEST AFRICA

THE **SAHARA** IS THE WORLD'S LARGEST DESERT, made up of over 9 million square kilometres of baking hot sand, gravel and rock.

Its northern fringes, occupied by **Morocco**, **Algeria**, **Tunisia** and **Libya**, run into the milder, more fertile lands of the Mediterranean coast and the Atlas mountain ranges. They are home to Arabs and Berbers.

Deserts stretch from the Sahara eastwards to **Egypt** and the Red Sea. In ancient times one of the greatest civilizations the world has seen grew up in Egypt. Then as now, the country depended on water from the world's longest

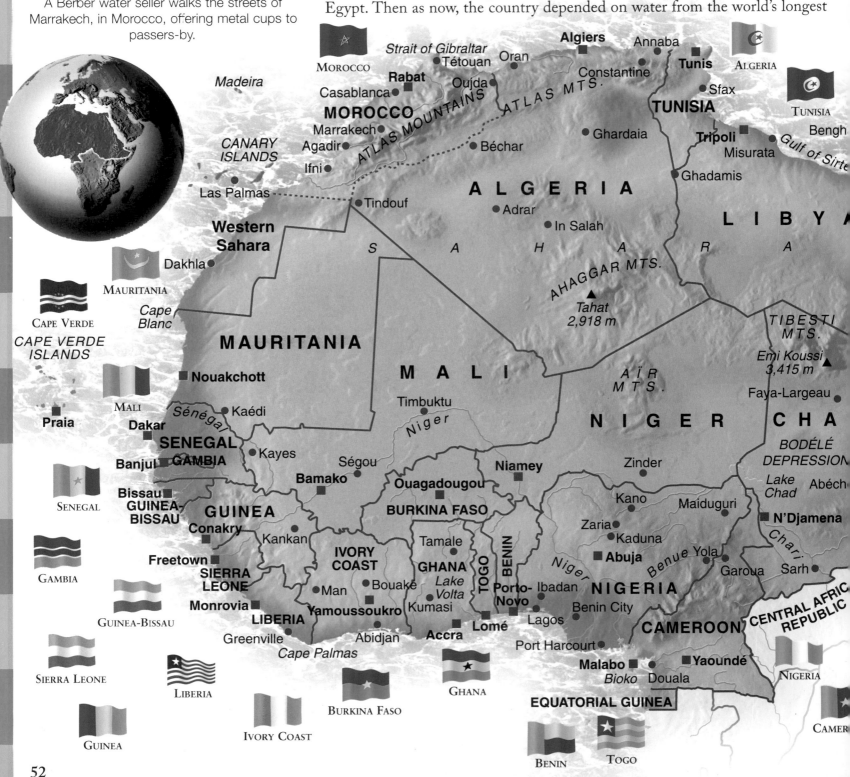

MOROCCO
Strait of Gibraltar
Oran
Algiers
Annaba
Tétouan
Tunis
ALGERIA
Rabat
Oujda
Constantine
Madeira
Casablanca
Sfax
MOROCCO
TUNISIA
TUNISIA
Marrakech
Ghardaia
Tripoli
Bengh
Agadir
Béchar
Misurata
Gulf of Sirte
CANARY
ISLANDS
Ifni
Ghadamis
ATLAS MOUNTAINS
ATLAS MTS.
Las Palmas
Tindouf
A L G E R I A
L I B Y A
Adrar
In Salah
Western
Sahara
S   A   H   A   R   A
AHAGGAR MTS.
Dakhla
▲ Tahat
2,918 m
TIBESTI
MTS.
MAURITANIA
Cape
Blanc
MAURITANIA
Emi Koussi
3,415 m
M A L I
AÏR
MTS.
Faya-Largeau
CAPE VERDE
CAPE VERDE
ISLANDS
Nouakchott
Timbuktu
N I G E R
C H A
BODÉLÉ
DEPRESSION
Niger
MALI
Kaédi
Sénégal
Lake
Chad
Abéch
Praia
Dakar
Zinder
SENEGAL
Kayes
Ségou
Niamey
Kano
Maiduguri
Banjul
GAMBIA
Bamako
Ouagadougou
N'Djamena
Bissau
GUINEA-
BISSAU
GUINEA
Conakry
BURKINA FASO
Zaria
Kaduna
Yola
SENEGAL
Kankan
Tamale
Abuja
Garoua
Sarh
GAMBIA
Freetown
IVORY
COAST
GHANA
TOGO
BENIN
Niger
NIGERIA
Benue
SIERRA
LEONE
Man
Bouaké
Lake
Volta
Porto-
Novo
Ibadan
GUINEA-BISSAU
Monrovia
Kumasi
Lagos
Benin City
CENTRAL AFRIC
REPUBLIC
SIERRA LEONE
LIBERIA
Yamoussoukro
Lomé
CAMEROON
Greenville
Abidjan
Accra
Port Harcourt
LIBERIA
Cape Palmas
Malabo
Yaoundé
NIGERIA
Bioko
Douala
BURKINA FASO
GHANA
CAMER
GUINEA
IVORY COAST
EQUATORIAL GUINEA
BENIN
TOGO

river, the Nile. This flows north to the Mediterranean from the mountains of **Ethiopia** and the swamps of southern **Sudan**, Africa's largest country.

The region south of the Sahara is known as the Sahel. It includes **Senegal**, **Mauritania**, **Mali**, **Niger**, **Burkina Faso** and **Chad**. The people include the Fulani, Kanuri and Hausa. The thin grasslands of the Sahel allow cattle herding, but droughts are common and the desert is spreading. Many people are very poor.

Thirteen nations border the great bulge of the West African coast, around the Gulf of Guinea. The coastal strip is made up of lagoons and long sandy beaches fringed with palm trees. Inland there is a belt of forest, which rises to dry, sandy plateaus and semi-desert in the far north. West African history tells of African kingdoms and empires which grew up here long ago, but also of the cruel slave trade across the Atlantic, which lasted from the 1500s to the 1800s. In the 1800s, large areas of West Africa became colonies of Britain and France. Today these lands are independent. The region has rich resources, including oil and diamonds.

Abu Simbel
When the new Aswan dam was being built in the 1960s this great temple of the ancient Egyptian ruler Rameses II had to be moved stone-by-stone.

Alexandria
Port Said
Suez
QATTARA Cairo Sinai
DEPRESSION Pen.
Asyût
Qena
EGYPT
Lake Aswân
Nasser
LIBYA
arnah
LIBYAN DESERT
Nubian Desert
Port Sudan
Merowe
Atbara
SUDAN
Kassala ERITREA
Omdurman Asmara
Khartoum Aksum
El Obeid ETHIOPIAN
al Marrah Kosti Lake Gonder
3,088 Tana PLATEAU
Debre Markos
Addis Ababa
SUDD
Gore
ETHIOPIA
Nimule
UGANDA KENYA
SOMALIA
DJIBOUTI
Djibouti
Ogaden
Webe Shebele
RIFT VALLEY
White Nile
Blue Nile
Nile
RED SEA
Atbara
EGYPT
ERITREA
DJIBOUTI
SUDAN
CHAD
ETHIOPIA
N

CENTRAL, EASTERN & SOUTHERN AFRICA

CENTRAL AFRICA is dominated by the river Congo, which flows through hot and humid rainforest to the Atlantic Ocean. The great river winds through the **Democratic Republic of the Congo**, and the network of waterways which drain into it provide useful transport routes for riverboats and canoes.

A long crack in the Earth's crust, the Great Rift Valley, runs all the way down **East Africa**. Its route is marked by volcanoes and lakes. Some East African mountains remain snow-capped all year round, even though they are on the Equator. The highest of these is Kilimanjaro, at 5,950 metres. It looks out over savanna, grasslands dotted with trees. Huge herds of wildlife roam these plains. Zebra, giraffe, elephants and lions are protected within national parks. The Indian Ocean coast includes white beaches and coral islands. Mombasa, Dar-es-Salaam and Maputo are major ports.

In southern Africa the Drakensberg mountains descend to grassland known as veld. There are harsh deserts too, the Kalahari and the Namib. The **Republic of South Africa** is one of the most powerful countries in Africa. It has ports at Durban and Capetown.

Central and southern Africa are rich in mineral resources, including gold, diamonds and copper. Eastern and southern Africa are important farming regions, raising cattle and producing coffee, vegetables, tropical fruits, tobacco, and grape vines.

African kingdoms flourished in the Congo region in the Middle Ages and the stone ruins of Great Zimbabwe recall gold traders of long ago. Today the region is home to hundreds of African peoples with many different languages and cultures.

Magnificent Masai
This young Masai girl wears her traditional beaded necklace and headdress. These noble, nomadic people herd cattle and live mainly in Kenya and Tanzania.

La Digue, Seychelles
Over 100 islands make up the Seychelles. La Digue is only 15 square kilometres in area, but the third most populated.

Cape Caseyr

• Berbera

SOMALIA

KENYA

UGANDA

ETHIOPIA

Lake
Turkana

KENYA

Juba

Mogadishu

Kisumu   Mt. Kenya
▲ 5,199 m

ke
oria   **Nairobi**

anza

• Kismayu

N

INDIAN OCEAN

▲
Kilimanjaro
5,895 m

• Mombasa

SOMALIA

odoma

• Zanzibar
Dar-es-Salaam

BURUNDI

SEYCHELLES

ANZANIA

Aldabra Is.

SEYCHELLES

Lake
Vyasa

C. Delgado

COMOROS

C. d'Ambre

LAWI

MALAWI

ngwe

• Moçambique

Antisiranana

MADAGASCAR

Blantyre

MOZAMBIQUE

Mahajanga

Mozambique Channel

Toamasina

MAURITIUS

eira

Antananarivo

MOZAMBIQUE

MADAGASCAR

MAURITIUS

Réunion
(France)

Fianarantsoa

ZIMBABWE

C. Ste. Marie

Sting in the tail
Scorpions always look threatening. The curled-forward tail contains a sting which can be deadly. They eat insects and other animals which they catch with their claws. They are most common in desert areas.

FACT BOX

◆ **Central African Republic**
Area: 624,975 sq km
Population: 3,300,000
Capital: Bangui
Main language: French
Currency: Franc CFA

◆ **Gabon**
Area: 267,665 sq km
Population: 1,200,000
Capital: Libreville
Main language: French
Currency: Franc CFA

◆ **Republic of Congo**
Area: 342,000 sq km
Population: 2,500,000
Capital: Brazzaville
Main language: French
Currency: Franc CFA

◆ **Democratic Republic of Congo (Zaïre)**
Area: 2,345,410 sq km
Population: 46,500,000
Capital: Kinshasa
Main language: French
Currency: Zaïre

◆ **Rwanda**
Area: 26,330 sq km
Population: 6,900,000
Capital: Kigali
Main languages: Kinyarwanda, French
Currency: Rwanda franc

◆ **Burundi**
Area: 27,835 sq km
Population: 5,900,000
Capital: Bujumbura
Main languages: Kirundi, French
Currency: Burundi franc

◆ **Uganda**
Area: 236,580 sq km
Population: 22,000,000
Capital: Kampala
Main language: English
Currency: Uganda shilling

◆ **Kenya**
Area: 582,645 sq km
Population: 28,200,000
Capital: Nairobi
Main languages: Swahili, English
Currency: Kenya shilling

◆ **Somalia**
Area: 630,000 sq km
Population: 9,500,000
Capital: Mogadishu
Main languages: Somali, Arabic
Currency: Somali shilling

◆ **Tanzania**
Area: 939,760 sq km
Population: 29,100,000
Capital: Dodoma
Main languages: Swahili, English
Currency: Tanzanian shilling

◆ **Seychelles**
Area: 404 sq km
Population: 100,000
Capital: Victoria
Official languages: English, French, Creole
Currency: Seychelles rupee

◆ **Comoros**
Area: 1,860 sq km
Population: 600,000
Capital: Moroni
Official languages: Arabic, French
Currency: Comorian franc

◆ **Mauritius**
Area: 1,865 sq km
Population: 1,100,000
Capital: Port Louis
Official language: English

◆ **Madagascar**
Area: 594,180 sq km
Population: 15,200,000
Capital: Antananarivo
Official languages: Malagasy, French
Currency: Malagasy franc

◆ **Mozambique**
Area: 784,755sq km
Population: 16,500,000
Capital: Maputo
Official language: Portuguese
Currency: Metical

◆ **Malawi**
Area: 94,080 sq km
Population: 9,500,000
Capital: Lilongwe
Official language: Chichewa, English
Currency: Kwacha

◆ **Zambia**
Area: 752,615 sq km
Population: 9,200,000
Capital: Lusaka
Official language: English
Currency: Kwacha

◆ **Zimbabwe**
Area: 390,310 sq km
Population: 11,500,000
Capital: Harare
Official language: English
Currency: Zimbabwe dollar

◆ **Botswana**
Area: 575,000 sq km
Population: 1,500,000
Capital: Gaborone
Official language: English
Currency: Pula

◆ **Lesotho**
Area: 30,345 sq km
Population: 2,100,000
Capital: Maseru
Official languages: Sesotho, English
Currency: Loti

◆ **Swaziland**
Area: 17,365 sq km
Population: 1,000,000
Capital: Mbabane
Official languages: Swazi, English
Currency: Lilangeni

◆ **South Africa**
Area: 1,220,845 sq km
Population: 44,500,000
Capitals: Pretoria, Cape Town
Official languages: Afrikaans, English, Ndebele, Sesotho, Swazi, Tsonga, Tswana, Venda, Xhodsa, Zulu
Currency: Rand

◆ **Namibia**
Area: 824,295 sq km
Population: 1,600,000
Capital: Windhoek
Official language: English
Currency: Namibian dollar

◆ **Angola**
Area: 1,246,700 sq km
Population: 11,500,000
Capital: Luanda
Official language: Portuguese
Currency: Kwanza

AUSTRALIA

THIS COUNTRY is the size of a continent, a huge mass of land surrounded by ocean. The heart of **Australia** is a vast expanse of baking desert, salt pans, shimmering plains and dry scrubland. Ancient, rounded rocks glow in the morning and evening sun.

These barren lands are fringed by grasslands, tropical forests, creeks and fertile farmland. In the far east is the Great Dividing Range, which rises to the high peaks of the Australian Alps. The southeast is crossed by the Murray and Darling rivers. The Great Barrier Reef, the world's largest coral reef, stretches for over 2,000 kilometres off the eastern coast, while the island of Tasmania lies to the south across the Bass Strait.

Most Australians don't live in the 'outback', the dusty back country with its huge sheep and cattle stations and its mines. They live in big coastal cities such as Brisbane, Sydney, Adelaide and Perth. There they enjoy a high standard of living, an outdoor lifestyle, sunshine and surfing.

To the many people who in recent years have come from Europe and Asia to settle in Australia, this seems like a new country. However it is really a very ancient land, cut off from other parts of the world so long that it has many animals seen nowhere else on Earth, such as kangaroos, echidnas and platypuses.

Australia has probably been home to Aboriginal peoples for over 50,000 years. European settlement began in 1788, when the British founded a prison colony at Botany Bay, near today's city of Sydney. Many Australians still like to keep in touch with British relatives and traditions, but the modern country follows its own path as one of the great economic powers of the Pacific region.

Opera on the harbour
Sydney's most famous landmark is its Opera House, built between 1959 and 1973. It rises from the blue waters of the harbour like a great sailing ship. Sydney, the capital of New South Wales, is Australia's biggest city with a population of about 3,700,000.

Christmas beetles
Australia and its surrounding islands are populated by many weird and wonderful insects and beetles. These beetles are from Christmas Island.

Aboriginal art
An Aboriginal artist from Groote Eylandt, an island in the Gulf of Carpentaria, completes a painting on bark. Paintings by Australia's Aborigines are admired around the world. They often recall the ancient myths and legends of their people, with bold, swirling patterns or pictures of animals.

Bonaparte Archipela
Broome
Fitzroy
Eighty Mile Beach
Port Hedland
De Grey
Barrow I.
Fortescue
Ashburton
Mt. Bruce
GIBSON DESER
Lake Macleod
Carnarvon
Murchison
Dirk Hartog I.
WESTERN AUSTRALI
Geraldton
Laverton
Kalgoorlie-Boulder
Perth
Fremantle
Bunbury
C. Naturaliste
Archipelago of th Recherche
C. Leeuwin
Albany

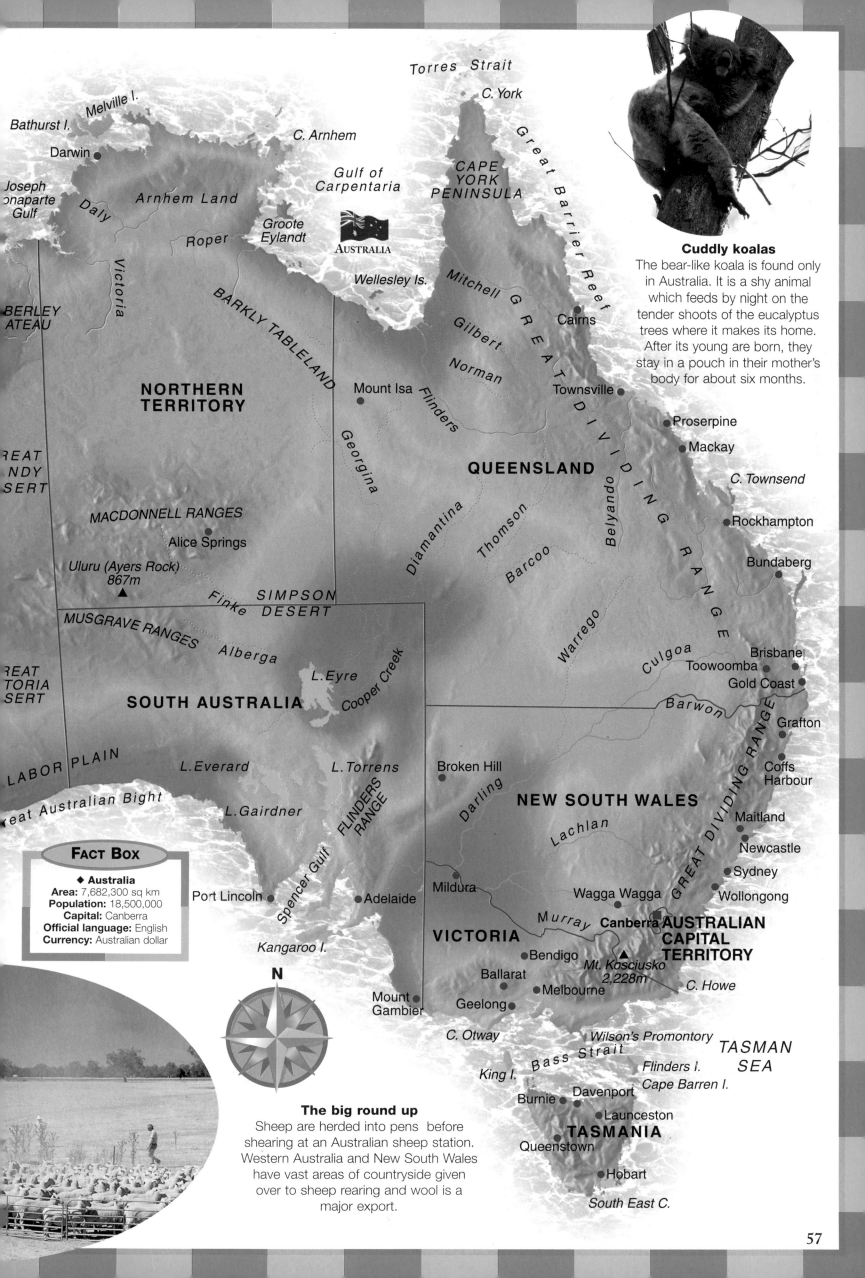

Torres Strait

C. York

Melville I.

Bathurst I.

Darwin

C. Arnhem

Gulf of
Carpentaria

CAPE
YORK
PENINSULA

Great Barrier Reef

Joseph
Bonaparte
Gulf

Arnhem Land

Daly

Roper

Groote
Eylandt

Victoria

Wellesley Is.

AUSTRALIA

Mitchell

GREAT

Cairns

BERLEY
ATEAU

BARKLY TABLELAND

NORTHERN
TERRITORY

Mount Isa

Gilbert

Norman

Flinders

Townsville

Proserpine

DIVIDING

Mackay

GREAT
NDY
SERT

Georgina

QUEENSLAND

C. Townsend

MACDONNELL RANGES

Alice Springs

Thomson

Diamantina

Barcoo

Belyando

RANGE

Rockhampton

Bundaberg

Uluru (Ayers Rock)
867m

GREAT
TORIA
SERT

SIMPSON
DESERT

MUSGRAVE RANGES

Finke

Alberga

Warrego

Culgoa

Brisbane
Toowoomba
Gold Coast

L.Eyre

Cooper Creek

SOUTH AUSTRALIA

Barwon

Grafton

LABOR PLAIN

L.Everard

L.Torrens

Broken Hill

FLINDERS RANGE

Darling

Coffs
Harbour

NEW SOUTH WALES

GREAT DIVIDING RANGE

Maitland

Newcastle

reat Australian Bight

L.Gairdner

Lachlan

Cuddly koalas
The bear-like koala is found only
in Australia. It is a shy animal
which feeds by night on the
tender shoots of the eucalyptus
trees where it makes its home.
After its young are born, they
stay in a pouch in their mother's
body for about six months.

Sydney

Port Lincoln

Spencer Gulf

Mildura

Wagga Wagga

Wollongong

Canberra AUSTRALIAN
CAPITAL
TERRITORY

FACT BOX
◆ **Australia**
Area: 7,682,300 sq km
Population: 18,500,000
Capital: Canberra
Official language: English
Currency: Australian dollar

Adelaide

Murray

VICTORIA

Bendigo

Mt. Kosciusko
2,228m

C. Howe

Kangaroo I.

Ballarat

Melbourne

N

Mount
Gambier

Geelong

C. Otway

Wilson's Promontory

TASMAN
SEA

King I.

Bass Strait

Flinders I.
Cape Barren I.

The big round up
Sheep are herded into pens before
shearing at an Australian sheep station.
Western Australia and New South Wales
have vast areas of countryside given
over to sheep rearing and wool is a
major export.

Burnie

Davenport

Launceston

TASMANIA

Queenstown

Hobart

South East C.

57

NEW ZEALAND AND THE PACIFIC

NEW ZEALAND LIES in the Pacific Ocean, about 1,600 kilometres to the east of Australia. It has a moist, mild climate and many unusual plants, birds and animals may be found there.

Most of its people live on North Island and South Island. These beautiful islands, divided by the Cook Strait, are the largest of several which are included within the country. North Island has volcanoes, hot springs and gushing geysers. South Island is dominated by the peaks and glaciers of the Southern Alps. It also has deep sea inlets called fiords and rolling grassy plains. New Zealand, with its sheep, cattle and fruit farms, has one of the most important economies in the Pacific region.

Papua New Guinea is another island nation, bordering Indonesian territory on the island of New Guinea. It also includes several chains of smaller islands. Many of its mountain regions, blanketed in tropical forests, were only opened up to the outside world in the 20th century. The country is rich in mineral resources and its fertile soils produce coffee, tea and rubber.

Strung out eastwards across the lonely Pacific Ocean are many scattered island chains and reefs. Small coral islands surround peaceful blue lagoons ringed with palm trees. The islanders may make their living by fishing, growing coconuts, mining or tourism. Many of the island groups have banded together to form independent nation states.

Peoples of the Pacific are of varied descent. Some are the descendants of European settlers – for example the British in New Zealand, or the French on New Caledonia or Tahiti. Fiji has a large population of Indian descent. The original peoples of the Pacific fall into three main groups. Melanesians, such as the Solomon Islanders, live in the western Pacific, while Micronesians live in the Caroline and Marshall Islands. The Polynesian peoples, brilliant seafarers, colonized vast areas of the ocean, from New Zealand to the Hawaiian Islands. The Maoris, who make up nine percent of New Zealand's population, are a Polynesian people who have kept and valued many of their ancient traditions.

MICRONESIA

SOLOMON ISLANDS

SEA OF JAPAN

Yellow Sea

East China Sea

Northern Mariana Islands (USA)

Guam (USA)

Federated States of Micronesia

Palau

SOUTH CHINA SEA

Philippine Sea

Celebes Sea

Papua New Guinea

Irian Jaya (Indonesia)

Arafura Sea

Port Moresby

Solomon Island

Coral Sea

AUSTRALIA

TASMAN SEA

New Guinea finery
Feathers and paint are worn by many young warriors at tribal gatherings and feasts in remote areas of Papua New Guinea. The country has a very rich culture with over 860 different languages.

Kiwi fruit
When farmers decided to grow this fruit in New Zealand, they decided to give it a local name to help sales. The kiwi is the national bird, and a nickname for a New Zealander.

BERING SEA

PAPUA NEW
GUINEA

PALAU

NORTH
PACIFIC
OCEAN

Midway Island
(USA)

Wake Island
(USA)

Hawaii (USA)

VANUATU

MARSHALL
ISLANDS

Marshall Island

KIRIBATI

Nauru

NAURU

Kiribati

Tuvalu

TUVALU

SAMOA

Galapagos
(Ecuador)

SOUTH
PACIFIC
OCEAN

Vanuatu

Samoa   American
Samoa

Fiji

French
Polynesia

New Caledonia
(France)

Cook Islands
(New Zealand)

Pitcairn Island
(UK)

Tonga

Easter Island
(Chile)

FIJI

TONGA

NEW ZEALAND

NEW
ZEALAND

FACT BOX

◆ **Papua New Guinea**
Area: 462,840 sq km
Population: 4,400,000
Capital: Port Moresby
Official language: English
Currency: Kina

◆ **New Zealand**
Area: 265,150 sq km
Population: 3,600,000
Capital: Auckland
Official language: English
Currency: New Zealand dollar

◆ **Palau**
Area: 490 sq km
Population: 16,000
Capital: Koror
Official languages: Palauan, English
Currency: US dollar

◆ **Marshall Islands**
Area: 181 sq km
Population: 52,000
Capital: Majuro
Official language: Marshallese, English
Currency: US dollar

◆ **Solomon Islands**
Area: 29,790 sq km
Population: 354,000
Capital: Honiara
Official language: English
Currency: Solomon Islands dollar

◆ **Tuvalu**
Area: 25 sq km
Population: 13,000
Capital: Funafuti
Official languages: Tuvaluan, English
Currency: Australian dollar

◆ **Kiribati**
Area: 684 sq km
Population: 75,000
Capital: Bairiki
Official language: English
Currency: Australian dollar

◆ **Nauru**
Area: 21 sq km
Population: 10,000
Capital: Yaren
Official language: Nauruan
Currency: Australian dollar

◆ **Fiji**
Area: 18,330 sq km
Population: 758,000
Capital: Suva
Official language: English
Currency: Fiji dollar

◆ **Tonga**
Area: 699 sq km
Population: 103,000
Capital: Nukualofa
Official languages: Tongan, English
Currency: Pa'anga

◆ **Vanuatu**
Area: 14,765 sq km
Population: 156,000
Capital: Porta-Vila
Official languages: Bislama, English, French
Currency: Vatu

◆ **Western Samoa**
Area: 2,840 sq km
Population: 170,000
Capital: Apia
Official languages: Samoan, English
Currency: Tala

◆ **Federated States of Micronesia**
Area: 702 sq km
Population: 114,000
Capital: Kolonia
Official language: English
Currency: US dollar

Easter Island

Hundreds of huge, mysterious stone heads tower above the hills of Easter Island, in the eastern Pacific. They were erected by Polynesians about 1,000 years ago. Today Easter Island is governed by Chile.

Gusher!

Steam bursts from volcanic rocks near Rotorua on North Island. New Zealand's geysers and hot springs are not just a tourist attraction. They are used to generate electricity.

NEW ZEALAND

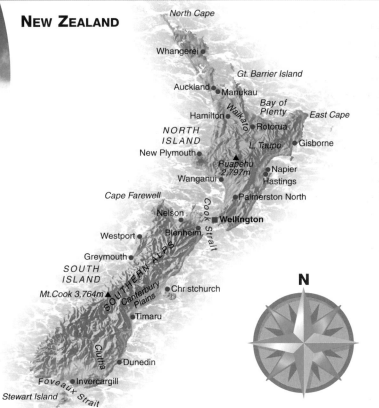

North Cape

Whangerei

Gt. Barrier Island

Auckland ● Manukau

Bay of Plenty

East Cape

Hamilton ● Waikato ● Rotorua

NORTH ISLAND

L. Taupo ● Gisborne

New Plymouth ●

Ruapehu 2,797m

● Napier

Wanganui ●

● Hastings

Cape Farewell

● Palmerston North

Nelson ●

Cook Strait

Wellington

Westport ●

● Blenheim

Greymouth ●

SOUTHERN ALPS

SOUTH ISLAND

Mt.Cook 3,764m

Canterbury Plains

● Christchurch

● Timaru

Clutha

● Dunedin

Foveaux Strait ● Invercargill

Stewart Island

N

POLAR LANDS

Living in the Arctic
The Inuit peoples of northern Canada and Greenland have always lived by hunting and fishing and are experts at surviving in the harsh climate.

THE NORTHERNMOST PART of our globe is called the Arctic. Within this bitterly cold region lie the northern borders of Alaska (part of the United States), Canada, Greenland (a self-governing territory of Denmark), Norway, Sweden, Finland and Russia.

However most of the area is covered by the Arctic Ocean, much of which is frozen solid all year round. At the centre of this great cap of ice is the North Pole. The **Arctic** supports a surprisingly wide selection of wildlife, including seals, walruses and polar bears. Peoples who have learned to live permanently in the far north include the Aleuts, the Inuit, the Saami, the Yakuts and the Chukchi. They have been joined in recent years by workers from the oil industry.

The only people to be found in **Antarctica**, at the other end of the globe, are scientists studying the weather and rocks of the coldest and windiest continent on Earth. The only other living things to survive here are the penguins which breed around the coast and the whales, birds and fishes of the Southern Ocean. The landmass is ringed by a shelf of ice, some of which breaks away to form massive icebergs in the spring. Inland there are mountain ranges and icy plains. The Antarctic winter takes place during the Arctic summer, and the Antarctic summer during the Arctic winter.

Various countries claim territory in Antarctica, and the continent is rich in minerals and fishing. However many scientists argue that this land should never be opened up to mining and industry, but left as the planet's last true wilderness.

Antarctic melt
Each southern spring, the ice around Antarctica begins to melt, allowing ships to approach the ice shelves around this huge, frozen continent.

FACT BOX
- ◆ Arctic Circle
  Area of ocean:
  14,056,000 sq km
- ◆ Antarctic Circle
  Area of land:
  13,900,000 sq km

INDEX

INDEX

Page numbers in *italics* refer to illustrations.

The publishers wish
to thank the artists
who have contributed
to this book:
Julie Banyard; Martin
Camm; Mike Foster;
Josephine Martin;
Terry Riley; Guy
Smith; Roger Smith;
Michael
White/Temple
Rogers.

The publishers would
like to thank the
following for
supplying
photographs for the
Atlas

Page 5 (T/R) MKP; 5
(B) PhotoDisc; 6-7,
9, 10-11 all MKP; 12
(C/R) & (B/L)
Spectrum Colour
Library; 14 (T/R)
MKP; (B/L) & (B)
The Stock Market; 15
(B) MKP; 17 (C/R)
& B/R) The Stock
Market; (B) MKP; 18
(B) MKP; (T/R) &
(B/R) The Stock
Market; 20-21, 24-25
all MKP; 26 (T/C)
MKP; (B/C) The
Stock Market; 28
(B/C) The Stock
Market; 29 (T/R)
The Stock Market; 30
both MKP; 32-33 (C)
MKP; 33 (C) The
Stock Market; 33
(B/R); MKP; 34
(T/L) MKP; 34 (B)
The Stock Market; 35
(C) MKP; 37 (T/L)
The Stock Market;
(B/C) PhotoDisc; 38
(B/L) MKP; 39
(T/R) PhotoDisc; (C)
& (B/R) The Stock
Market; 40-41 all Sue
Cunningham
Photographic; 42-43
all MKP; 44 (T/L)
MKP; 45 (C/R) The
Stock Market; (B)
MKP; 46 (T/R) The
Stock Market; (B) &
(B/C) MKP; 47
(C/R) MKP; 48
(T/R) & (C) MKP;
49 (C/R) MKP;
(B/C) The Stock
Market; 50-51 all
MKP; 52-53 all
MKP; 54-55 all The
Stock Market; 56
(T/R) & (B/L) MKP;
(B/C) The Stock
Market; 58-59, 60-61
all MKP

64